Mindfulness and Thoughtfulness

Mindfulness and Thoughtfulness

Leading and Teaching with Habits of Mind in Research and Practice

Edited by

Servet Altan and Jennie Farber Lane

ROWMAN & LITTLEFIELD
Lanham • Boulder • New York • London

Published by Rowman & Littlefield
An imprint of The Rowman & Littlefield Publishing Group, Inc.
4501 Forbes Boulevard, Suite 200, Lanham, Maryland 20706
www.rowman.com

86-90 Paul Street, London EC2A 4NE, United Kingdom

British Library Cataloguing in Publication Information Available

Library of Congress Cataloging-in-Publication Data

Names: Altan, Servet, 1983– editor.
Title: Mindfulness and thoughtfulness : leading and teaching with habits of mind in research and practice / Edited by Servet Altan and Jennie Farber Lane.
Description: Lanham, Maryland : Rowman & Littlefield Publishing Group, [2023] | Includes bibliographical references. | Summary: "Essential for teachers and students to develop critical thinking skills is examining current dispositions and behaviors; to become more mindful of why we think the way we do and to become more thoughtful about actions we take. Mindfulness and Thoughtfulness provides both theoretical basis for, and practical ideas about, the Habits of Mind"— Provided by publisher.
Identifiers: LCCN 2022049213 (print) | LCCN 2022049214 (ebook) | ISBN 9781475869453 (cloth) | ISBN 9781475869460 (paperback) | ISBN 9781475869477 (epub)
Subjects: LCSH: Reflective learning. | Mindfulness (Psychology) | Critical thinking— Study and teaching. | Effective teaching. | Educational leadership.
Classification: LCC LB1027.23 .M56 2023 (print) | LCC LB1027.23 (ebook) | DDC 370.15/2--dc23/eng/20221129
LC record available at https://lccn.loc.gov/2022049213
LC ebook record available at https://lccn.loc.gov/2022049214

We thank our parents for their wisdom and care which helped us develop our Habits of Mind. We thank Erskine Dottin for inspiring the thoughtful and mindful approach we are using.

Servet & Jennie

Contents

Foreword

"The greatest discovery of any generation is that human beings can alter their lives by altering the attitudes of their minds."

—Albert Schweitzer, M.D.

We are living in an era of increasing volatility, uncertainty, complexity, and ambiguity, in which we are bombarded with conflicting models of what to value, what to believe, how to make decisions, and how to live productively. When students were asked for the three words that best described their emotional feelings, 80 percent said "stressed," "bored," and "tired" (Brackett, 2017). Further research showed students, teachers, and others in the workforce predominantly used the same words. Our brains are wired for consistency, yet we are experiencing constant disruption of what we have come to expect, and this uncertainty is causing us stress and malaise.

THE CENTRALITY OF THINKING DISPOSITIONS

Our society needs citizens who are well informed, skillful, and compassionate thinkers: people who have the disposition to value truth, openness, creativity, and interdependence. Education plays a central role in cultivating these traits by how they are designing their curriculum, choosing what is essential to teach, and creating learning environments that are flexible enough to adapt and accommodate to a rapidly changing world. The authors of this book introduce us to pathways toward developing such a school culture in which thinking dispositions, 16 Habits of Mind, are researched and intentionally taught, learned, and assessed.

Growing Dispositions

Human beings, to the best of our knowledge, are the only form of life with the capacity for metacognition—the ability to stand off and examine our own thoughts while we engage in them. Although the human brain is able to generate reflective consciousness, not everyone seems to use it equally (Csikszentmihalyi, 1993). As a result, everyone in education needs to engage with a curriculum that challenges our thinking.

Thinking involves the whole of us: our emotions, our ways of feeling in the body, our ideas, our beliefs, our qualities of character and our visions of being. Learning to think begins with consciously recognizing how we are thinking in the moment. We can begin to think by listening first to ourselves and to our own reactions; to learn to watch how our thoughts encapsulate us. When confronted with problematic situations we all must learn to habitually monitor our reactions by asking ourselves:

- What is the most intelligent action I can take right now?
- How can I learn from this? What are my resources? How can I draw on my past successes with problems by considering: What do I already know about the problem? What resources do I have available or need to generate?
- How can I approach this problem flexibly? How might I look at the situation in another way? How can I look at this problem from a fresh perspective? Am I remaining open to new possibilities and learnings?
- How can I illuminate this problem to make it clearer, more precise? Do I need to check out my data sources? How might I break this problem down into its component parts and develop a strategy for understanding and accomplishing each step?
- What do I know or not know? What questions do I need to ask? What strategies are in my mind now? What am I aware of in terms of my own beliefs, values, and goals with this problem? What feelings or emotions am I aware of which might be blocking or enhancing my progress?
- How is this problem affecting others? How can we solve it together and what can I learn from others that would help me become a better problem solver?

Each of these questions triggers a Habit of Mind and, over time, asking questions like this becomes a way of thinking. It becomes a habit.

Teachers can cause students to reflect on their own thoughtfulness by posing challenging problems and then having students describe their plans and strategies for solving the problem, sharing their thinking as they are implementing their plan, and then reflectively evaluating the effectiveness of the strategy that they employed.

Making Sense of Learning

The brain's capacity and desire to make or elicit patterns of meaning is one of the keys of brain-based learning. We never really understand something until we can create a model or metaphor derived from our unique personal world. The reality we perceive, feel, see, and hear is influenced by the constructive processes of the brain as well as by the cues that impinge upon it. It is not the content stored in memory but the activity of constructing it that gets stored. Humans don't *get* ideas; they *make* ideas.

Learning of content, therefore, should not be viewed as an end of instruction, but rather as a vehicle for activating and engaging the mind. Content is selected to serve as a vehicle for experiencing the joy ride of learning. We socially construct meaning by reaching out to others, subscribing to networks in which we gather other's perspectives, and we engage in a reciprocal process in which the individual influences the group and the group influences the individual.

BUILDING THE SCHOOL CULTURE AS A HOME FOR THINKING

In order for students to be committed to learning, they need to be in schools that are learning organizations. Key to the belief that everyone can contribute and help to grow the organization is a concomitant belief that all people can become more motivated and skillful thinkers. Successful leaders know the benefits of effective thinking and are alert to situational cues that signal when it counts; they are conscious of their own mental energies and problem-solving strategies; they know when it is appropriate to use skillful thinking and they reflect on and continually strive to improve their cognitive processes. A "good" thinker is not only skillful but also inclined, disposed, and compelled to employ patterns of effective thought (Costa & Kallick, 2020).

Thinking Big and Long Range

Attention to dispositions is powerfully emerging around the world. For example, ministries of education as well as leading business organizations in many nations suggest the following essentials (Mansilla & Jackson, 2011):

- Investigating the world beyond our immediate environment

- Recognizing our own and others' perspectives
- Communicating ideas effectively with diverse audiences
- Translating ideas and findings into appropriate actions to improve conditions

These essentials require certain propensities, inclinations or tendencies, such as:

- *Being curious*: wondering, questioning and problem posing
- *Taking risks*: persisting, striving for accuracy
- *Empathizing with others*: collaborating, inhibiting impulse, listening
- *Thinking flexibly*: communicating with clarity, both orally and in writing

Furthermore, we are finally realizing that every individual has the right to have their intellect developed to the fullest potential and that the human brain can continue to develop throughout one's lifetime (Boaler, 2019). As we create this highly personalized learning environment, we suggest that the Habits of Mind becomes a learning organization's fundamental set of behaviors that define the culture.

Thus, the Habits of Mind serves a larger, more spiritual agenda: To build a more thoughtful world as an interdependent learning community where all people are continually searching for ways to trust each other, to learn together, and to grow toward greater intelligence. By caring for and learning from one another and sharing the riches and resources in one part of the globe to help the less fortunate others achieve their fullest intellectual potential:

- A world community which strives to generate more thoughtful approaches to solving problems in peaceful ways.
- A world community that values human diversity of other cultures, races, religions, language systems, time perspectives, and political and economic views in an effort to bring about harmony and stability.
- A world of greater consciousness of our human effects on each other and on the earth's limited resources in an effort to live more respectfully, graciously, and harmoniously in our delicate environment.
- A world of better communication with other peoples, regardless of what language they speak, to employ clear and respectful dialogue.

When teachers support students to "think big" they inquire into such moral, ethical, and spiritual questions concerned with what makes human beings human; what is beauty, what is good, and what is just. The Habits of Mind, therefore, supports a vision of classrooms, schools, and communities and, indeed, a world that is more thoughtful.

"The best way to predict the future is to invent it," said Alan Kay, Apple Computer Co. If we want a future that is much more thoughtful, vastly more cooperative, greatly more compassionate, and a lot more loving, then we have to invent it. The future is in our schools and classrooms today.

Arthur L. Costa
Granite Bay, California
Bena Kallick
Westport, Connecticut

Preface

It was December 2019 when we heard about the first COVID-19 cases in Asia. At the time, it was not known to what extent this new virus would affect the whole world. Soon after, it turned into a global pandemic; while it had unprecedented effects on all walks of life, and surely one of the most affected institutions was schools.

The pandemic changed the rhythm of life for everyone. Precautions were taken to slow down its spread; in most countries, schools moved their teaching platforms to digital learning spaces, and this continued to be the case for a long time. For most, emergency remote teaching (ERT) felt like being "thrown into the sea without knowing how to swim." Teachers needed to work from home and manage their work and home responsibilities simultaneously. Even experienced practitioners reported they felt like novice teachers having to learn all over again how to make education effective and meaningful. Unfortunately, many teachers reported increased levels of stress, and at times the joy of teaching seemed to evade them.

ERT also affected students. The education of 1.6 billion students, or about half of the students at all levels of education, were disrupted by the closure of educational institutions and the interruption of face-to-face teaching (UNESCO, 2020a; UNESCO, 2020b). In some places, students were not able to access to any kind of education and the achievement gap between those who could and could not access education increased. While precautions such as quarantine, self-isolation and maintaining social distance successfully helped to reduce the spread of COVID-19, students were missing something essential: the human connection. Connections with their teachers, their peers, hands-on resources, and an interactive learning environment.

Although schools have generally gone back to face-to-face instruction, students and teachers still feel the effects of ERT. Moreover, many of us know we will face other crises—local or global—that will affect "normal" teaching. Actually, we are beginning to realize not only is there a new normal, but the concept of normal may be limited and impractical. While experiencing this turbulence across the world, we realized how important it is for all (especially students and teachers in this context) to develop the Habits of Mind that would help us develop dispositions to face and handle situations for which we do not yet have answers. The COVID-19 pandemic has reminded us of the importance of developing mindful and thoughtful ways of thinking that can help us face our everyday and unique crises and opportunities.

Recognizing the need to help educators identify and develop mindful and thoughtful teaching dispositions is why we started this project. We reached out to Habits of Mind researchers, practitioners, and educators from all over the world to create a valuable collection of research-based and practical ideas for teachers (pre-service, in-service), teacher educators, and teacher education programs. Based on Costa and Kallick's decades of experience with Habits of Mind, this book offers guidance to educators and parents on ways to cultivate these important dispositions. We believe that when dispositions are perceived as malleable traits rather than fixed entities; therefore, we hope the suggestions and practices from this book can help us develop desired Habits of Mind and lead to mindful and thoughtful ways of thinking, knowing, and being.

REFERENCES

UNESCO. (2020a). *School closures caused by Coronavirus (Covid-19).* UNESCO. https://en.unesco.org/covid19/educationresponse
UNESCO. (2020b). *Startling digital divides in distance learning emerge.* UNESCO. https://en.unesco.org/news/startling-digital-divides-distance-learning-emerge

Acknowledgments

We wish to express our appreciation to the many contributors to this book. The descriptions of their research, experiences, lessons, implementation and assessment strategies, and vignettes have made this book unique for educators, pedagogical leaders, researchers of the Habits of Mind (HoM) and to many others. The research in this book lays the foundation for the Habits of Mind and the experiences, instructional strategies and personal examples inspire and bring the Habits of Mind to life with many practical examples. The examples and tools encourage educators' and students' growth as well as schoolwide implementation of the 16 Habits of Mind.

We pay particular tribute to Art Costa and Bena Kallick, whose wisdom, research, and guidance of the 16 Habits of Mind have guided us on ways to cultivate these important dispositions. To them we are grateful. We express sincere gratitude to all contributing authors for their ideas and expertise. We appreciate their willingness to collaborate, revise and update their chapters in response to our reviews. We also pay particular tribute to Erskine Dottin, who helped us grow in our journey with experiencing the Habits of Mind. We wish to thank Tom Koerner, Kira Hall, and other members of the Rowman & Littlefield publishing staff who encouraged and guided us throughout this project.

Finally, we wish to acknowledge the many teachers, administrators, and parents in the numerous schools and communities thoughout the world who have adopted and implemented the Habits of Mind and have found them a meaningful way to organize learning and teaching. The future world will be a more thoughtful, compassionate, and cooperative place because of more mindful and thoughtful education practices through HoM that provide students with meaningful and constructive learning experiences.

Introduction

This book, *Mindfulness and Thoughtfulness: Leading and Teaching with Habits of Mind in Research and Practice,* brings a unique perspective to Habits of Mind (HoM) by focusing on two important and timely concepts for teachers today: mindfulness and thoughtfulness. These concepts are needed in a world where teachers may be overwhelmed when helping their students face global and regional issues such as climate change, social justice, and threats to health and well-being.

Cultivating HoM leads to intelligent behaviors that constructively and flexibly improve teaching practices. Practices that can help students develop knowledge, dispositions, and skills they will need to ensure a sustainable world for today and tomorrow.

This book provides teachers, curriculum developers, and professional development providers with a deeper and clearer understanding of dispositions, an important concept in teacher education. A variety of researchers and educators present learning theories, case studies, teaching techniques and professional development strategies associated with Habits of Mind and the concepts of mindfulness and thoughtfulness. The book is organized into three parts.

- *Part I: Discovering Mindful and Thoughtful Habits of Mind for Effective Teaching: What Does the Research Suggest?* researches into learning theories associated with Habits of Minds that helps explain intelligent behaviors and associated dispositions.
- *Part II: Creating Thoughtful and Mindful School Culture and Curriculum with Habits of Mind* includes chapters that provide recommendations and strategies for ensuring that HoM are integrated into the school setting as a whole (its mission, profile and curriculum).
- *Part III: Teaching and Assessing Habits of Mind* showcases professional development experiences and case studies that share how HoM have been implemented, developed, and assessed.

All three parts provide readers with the background, design strategies, and awareness of how to implement more mindful and thoughtful education practices through HoM that provide students with meaningful and constructive learning experiences.

PART I

Discovering Mindful and Thoughtful Habits of Mind for Effective Teaching: What Does the Research Suggest?

Chapter 1

Discovering and Exploring
Habits of Mind

Allison Zmuda, Arthur L. Costa, and Bena Kallick

What are Habits of Mind? Where did they come from? And why are they important? This introductory chapter is intended to acquaint you with a set of powerful mental dispositions that are essential for productive and successful living today and in the future.

Derived from the studies of successful people in many walks of life, the Habits of Mind is a set of 16 thinking dispositions at the core of social, emotional, and cognitive behaviors (Costa & Kallick, 2008). These habits help us respond intelligently and empathically when confronted with problem situations, conflicts, and uncertainties the resolutions to which are not immediately apparent. Our hypothesis is that if these are the attributes of successful people, then how can we teach them to students so that they will be successful in life as well? And if students learn them, might we create a more mindful and thoughtful world culture?

WHY ARE THE HABITS OF MIND IMPORTANT
NOW AND IN THE FUTURE?

While we are uncertain of just how it will ultimately unfold, we are in the midst of a technological revolution that is altering the way we live, work, and relate to one another. Our inventions and innovations are continuously changing our world. In its scale, scope, and complexity, the transformation will be unlike anything humankind has experienced before. This revolution will affect all peoples of the world. We will continue to be bombarded with

3

complex and conflicting models of what to value, what to believe, how to make decisions and how to live productively (Schwab, 2016).

Numerous international authoritative futurists, neuroscientists, educators, and sociologists point to the need for problem solving, creating, innovating, and communicating in order to sustain the societies in which we live (Lieberman, 2021). They include in their list *dispositions* that are essential to learning.

FROM WHENCE THEY CAME?

In 1984, recognizing the central role that thinking would play in addressing this transforming world, Art was invited by ASCD to edit a book, *Developing Minds: A Resource Book for Teaching Thinking*. For that first edition, as well as subsequent second and third editions (1991 & 2001), he invited authorities from around the world in the fields of cognition, psychology, education, and philosophy to describe the attributes of effective problem solvers and decision makers in many walks of life.

As he read each author's contribution, he began to see some recurring patterns and themes. While each writer approached their topic from a different perspective and had different labels, their intentions were similar. They wrote about being flexible and open-minded in thinking, monitoring one's own thoughts and actions, being curious and having a questioning attitude. As he continued his research in the fields of cognitive psychology, emotional intelligence, and neuroscience, he observed that there were common attributes or dispositions that appeared repeatedly.

With Bena Kallick as co-editor, they adopted the term, "Habits of Mind," and published their seminal book *Learning and Leading with Habits of Mind* (2008). Wanting to communicate the Habits as actionable they ensured that all the Habits of Mind were stated as verbs ending with -ing. So, for example, rather than using terms such as "communication," they listed the Habits and behaviors that would promote effective communication such as: listening with understanding and empathy or questioning and posing problems. The practicality of the book resonated with educators and has been translated into several other languages. The Habits of Mind have spread to schools throughout the United States and around the world.

Substantial research is being collected (although more is needed) which indicates that students prosper intellectually, socially, and emotionally as they learn the Habits of Mind. Teachers form stronger bonds with their colleagues when they use the Habits in their collaborative work, schools develop a culture of mindfulness, and individual teachers report renewed dedication, energy, and excitement about their teaching (Edwards, 2014). All this takes time, however. The Habits are as good for adults as they are for students. All of us can get better at the Habits of Mind. And that is what gives the Habits of Mind dignity regardless of whatever challenges we face in the future.

WHAT ARE THESE 16 HABITS OF MIND?

While we have numbered the Habits of Mind below, the sequence is not intended to communicate their importance or any particular sequence of introducing them. We did however, isolate our description of metacognition and list it first because metacognition is the "Executive Director"—the "GPS" of all the other Habits of Mind.

1. *Thinking about your thinking* (Metacognition) means being aware of and regulating your own thoughts, strategies, feelings, and actions and their effects on others. Occurring in the neocortex of the brain, metacognition is the capacity to monitor and control our cognitive processes (executive functions) and mental habits. It is our ability to know what we know and what we don't know, to plan a strategy for producing what information is needed, to be conscious of our own steps and strategies during the act of problem solving, and to reflect on and evaluate the productiveness of our own thinking.

The major components of metacognition include:

- *Developing a plan of action.* Forming goals and outcomes and planning a strategy before embarking on a course of action assists us in keeping track of the steps in the sequence of planned behavior at the conscious, awareness level for the duration of the activity.
- *Making temporal and comparative judgments.* Assessing the readiness for more or different activities and monitoring our interpretations, perceptions, decisions, and behaviors.
- *Having an inner dialogue (self-talk).* This includes mental rehearsal, inner-coaching, and self-questioning. Our "inner voice" is what we use to reflect on what we do; how and why we behave the way we do; how we critique ourselves; and how we connect the knowledge and ideas into conceptual frameworks.

Thoughtful people plan for, reflect on, and evaluate the quality of their own thinking skills and strategies. Through metacognition, we become increasingly aware of our actions and the effect of those actions on others and on the environment. We form internal questions as we search for information and meaning, developing mental maps or plans of action. We mentally rehearse prior to performance, monitoring those plans as they are employed, being conscious of the need for midcourse correction if the plan is not meeting expectations. Throughout this process we develop a mental picture of our outcomes and continually revise our plan based on experience. Upon completion, we reflect on the plan for the purpose of self-evaluation.

2. *Persisting* means persevering with a task through to completion; remaining focused and searching for ways to reach your goal when stuck; not giving up. Persisting has a dramatic impact on successful problem solving. Ineffective problem solvers often give up when the answer to a problem is not immediately known. They sometimes say, "I can't do this," "It's too hard," or they accept any answer to get the task over with. Some have difficulty staying focused for any length of time. They are easily distracted and lack the ability to analyze a problem and to develop a system, structure, or strategy of problem attack. They may give up because they have a limited repertoire of problem-solving strategies—when their strategy doesn't work, they give up because they have no alternatives.

Efficacious people, however, stick to a task until it is completed. They don't give up easily. They analyze a problem and develop a system, structure, or strategy in which to attack a problem. They employ a range and have a repertoire of alternative strategies for problem solving. They collect evidence to indicate their problem-solving strategy is working, and, if one strategy doesn't work, they know how to back up and try another. They recognize when a theory or idea must be rejected and another employed. They have systematic methods of analyzing a problem which include knowing how to begin, knowing what steps must be performed, and knowing what data need to be generated or collected.

Persisting is central to any problem-solving process. When faced with ambiguous situations or uncertain situations, we learn how to generate and test multiple solution paths. We often become more creative as we work through the frustration and confusion of finding alternative problem-solving strategies.

3. *Managing impulsivity* means thinking before acting; remaining calm, thoughtful, and deliberative. Effective thinkers have a sense of deliberativeness: they think before they act. They intentionally form a vision of a product, plan of action, goal, or destination before they begin. They strive to clarify and understand directions, develop a strategy for approaching a problem, and withhold immediate value judgments before fully understanding an idea. As reflective individuals, they consider alternatives and consequences of several possible directions prior to taking action. They decrease their need for trial and error by gathering information, taking time to reflect on an answer before giving it, making sure they understand directions, and listening to alternative points of view.

Impulsive people sometimes adopt the first answer that comes to mind, start to work without fully understanding the directions, and lack an organized plan or strategy for approaching a problem. They may take the first suggestion given or operate on the most obvious and simple idea that comes to mind rather than considering more complex alternatives and consequences of several possible directions.

4. *Striving for accuracy* means doing your best, setting high standards, fact checking, and finding ways to improve constantly. People who value accuracy, precision, and craftsmanship take time to check over their products. They review the rules by which they abide, revisit the models and visions they are to follow, and confirm that their finished product matches the criteria for quality exactly. They take pride in their accomplishments, so they take time to check over their work. They exhibit craftsman-like behaviors such as exactness, precision, correctness, faithfulness, and fidelity. They also take time to certify the products of others. Rather than merely accepting information at face value, they distinguish between facts and opinions as they search for the most accurate information. They are critical thinkers who are alert to checking the truth or falsity of news and other claims found in social networking. They learn to recognize implicit bias in themselves as well as in others.

5. *Thinking flexibly* means being able to change perspectives, generate alternatives, and consider options. An amazing discovery about the human brain is its plasticity—its ability to "rewire," change, and even repair itself. Neuroplasticity means that our brains can physically change to encourage creative thinking and new knowledge.

Cognitive flexibility is the cradle of humor, creativity, and repertoire. It helps us remain open and receptive to new experiences, multiple sources of information, a variety of interpretations, varied approaches to problems, and alternative points of view. Flexible thinkers have the capacity to change their mind as they receive additional data. They engage in multiple and simultaneous outcomes and activities, drawing upon a repertoire of problem-solving strategies. They practice style flexibility—knowing when it is appropriate to be broad and global in their thinking and when a situation requires detailed, analytic precision.

Flexible people approach problems from various angles using new and novel approaches. They consider alternative points of view and their minds are open to change based on additional information or reasoning even when it contradicts their original beliefs. Flexible thinkers know that they have and can develop options and alternatives to consider. They catch and correct errors. They understand and are being able to work within rules, criteria, and regulations, and they can predict the consequences of ignoring them. Flexibility of mind is essential for working with social diversity, enabling an individual to recognize and respect the wholeness and distinctness of other people's ways of experiencing and making meaning.

6. *Listening with understanding and empathy* means devoting mental energy to another person's thoughts and ideas; making an effort to perceive another's point of view and emotions. Highly effective people spend an inordinate amount of time and energy listening. Some psychologists believe that the ability to listen to another person, to empathize with, and to understand their point of view is one of the highest forms of intelligent behavior.

While we spend 55 percent of our lives listening, in actuality, we may not be listening as much as rehearsing in our head what we are going to say when the other person is finished. Poor listeners may ridicule, laugh at, or put down others' ideas. They often interrupt and are unable to build upon, consider the merits of, or operate on another person's ideas.

Effective listeners gently attend to another person by demonstrating their understanding of and empathy for their ideas or feelings. Indicators of effective, sincere listening include being able to paraphrase another person's ideas; detecting cues of their feelings or emotional states in their oral and body language; and accurately expressing the other person's concepts, emotions, and problems. They paraphrase accurately and build upon what was said by giving possible examples. They listen empathically by silencing the voices with themselves so that they can pay close attention to what is being said beneath the words and identify with the other's emotions and intentions.

Sincere listeners invest themselves in their partner's ideas. They hold in abeyance their own values, judgments, opinions, and prejudices in order to listen to and entertain the other person's thoughts. This is a very complex skill requiring the ability to monitor one's own thoughts while, at the same time, attending to their partner's words. This does not mean that they can't disagree with someone. A good listener tries to understand what the other person is saying. In the end, they may disagree sharply, but because they disagree, they want to know exactly what it is they are disagreeing with.

When listening with understanding and empathy, something quite surprising occurs: both the brain of the listener and the brain of the other person begin to align with one another. This special bond is a phenomenon referred to as "neural resonance" and, in this enhanced state of mutual attunement, two people can accomplish remarkable things together because it eliminates the natural defensiveness that normally exists when people casually converse.

7. *Questioning and posing problems* means having a questioning attitude, knowing what data are needed, and developing questioning strategies to produce those data. It also means *finding* problems to solve. When either asking or being asked a question, the brain becomes active. As we search for an answer, it releases serotonin, allowing it to relax. This encourages gathering intelligence from all areas of the brain, which stimulates even greater insight. New neuronal connections begin to be made as the brain searches to find solutions. As serotonin is released, a rush of energy (or insight) occurs as the

brain fires up, moving ahead and discovering the solutions to a problem. We become motivated and ready for action (Asmus, 2017).

One of the distinguishing characteristics between humans and other forms of life is our inclination and ability to *find* problems to solve. The drive to make sense of our environment, make inquiries, and uncover answers has been crucial to human survival. Curiosity is the desire for knowledge in the absence of extrinsic reward. When individuals feel curious, they engage in persistent information-seeking behavior. Curiosity has been recognized as a powerful motivator for not only learning but also creativity and subjective well-being. What sets effective thinkers apart is their passionate desire to contribute new knowledge and to find or invent better ways of living.

8. *Thinking interdependently* means working with and learning from others in reciprocal situations—teamwork. Human beings are social beings. We congregate in groups, find it therapeutic to be listened to, draw energy from one another, and seek reciprocity. In groups, we contribute our time and energy to tasks that we would quickly tire of when working alone. In fact, one of the cruelest forms of punishment that can be inflicted on an individual is solitary confinement.

Reflecting on our fundamentally inquisitive, social nature, humans try to understand what others are doing. In order to survive as a species, we learned to "read" the people around us so that we could collaborate, fight enemies, and find food. The social brain is always there, and it appears to be active very early in our development.

Interdependent humans realize that all of us together are more powerful, intellectually and physically, than any one individual. The foremost disposition in the post-industrial society is likely the heightened ability to think in concert with others; to become increasingly more interdependent and sensitive to the needs of others. Problem solving is so complex that no one person can go it alone. No one has access to all the data needed to make critical decisions; no one person can consider as many alternatives as several people can.

In addition to collaborating face-to-face with colleagues across a conference table, modern workers increasingly accomplish tasks through mediated interactions with peers halfway across the world whom they may never meet face-to-face. The importance of cooperative interpersonal capabilities requires even more sophistication than in the prior industrial era.

When working in groups, each individual must be open to accept critique or receive feedback from trusted others who share in their desire for all to be successful. Through this interaction, the group and the individual continue to grow. Listening, consensus seeking, giving up an idea to work with someone else's, empathy, compassion, group leadership, knowing how to support group efforts, and altruism are all behaviors indicative of thinking independently.

9. *Thinking and communicating with clarity and precision* means striving for accurate communication in both written and oral form; avoiding over-generalizations, distortions, deletions, and exaggerations. Language and thinking are closely entwined. Like either side of a coin, they are inseparable. When you hear fuzzy language, it is a reflection of fuzzy thinking or the desire for someone to deceive you with their fuzzy thinking. Thoughtful people strive to communicate accurately in both written and oral forms, taking care to use precise language, define terms, and use correct names and universal labels and analogies.

We sometimes hear others using vague and imprecise language. They describe objects or events with words like *weird, nice,* or *OK.* They label specific objects using such nondescriptive words as *stuff, junk,* and *things.* They punctuate sentences with meaningless interjections like *"ya know," "er,"* and *"uh."* They use vague or general nouns and pronouns: *"They* told me to do it," *"Everybody* has one," or *"Teachers* don't understand me." They use nonspecific verbs ("Let's *do* it") and unqualified comparatives ("This soda is *better*; I like it *more"*).

When people use language with greater specificity in both written and oral forms, it enhances another person's cognitive maps and their ability to think critically and plan for effective action. When writing or preparing for a presentation, people plan ahead by mentally rehearsing their messages. They think about what the main points are that they wish to convey and how they want to structure their presentation. Enriching the complexity and specificity of language simultaneously produces more effective thinking.

10. *Applying past knowledge to new situations* means accessing prior knowledge; transferring knowledge beyond the situation in which it was learned. Intelligent human beings learn from experience. When confronted with a new and perplexing problem they draw forth experience from their past. They can often be heard saying, "This reminds me of. . . . " or "This is just like the time when. . . . " They explain what they are doing now in terms of analogies or references to previous experiences.

They call upon their store of knowledge and experience as sources of data to support theories they are trying to explain or processes they might use to solve a problem or confront a new challenge. They are also able to abstract meaning from one experience and carry it forth so that they can apply it to new and novel situations.

Ineffective thinkers begin each new task as if it were being approached for the very first time. Their thinking is what Feuerstein et al. (1980) referred to as an "episodic grasp of reality." That is, each event in life is a separate and discrete event with no connections to what may have come before or with no relation to what follows. Their learning is so encapsulated that they seem unable to draw forth wisdom from one event and apply it in another context.

Efficacious thinkers, however, possess a fluid and accessible short and long term memory. They can:

- Store, recall, and manipulate visual and verbal information, including signals from the environment, directions, rules, graphics, images, and so on, compare and contrast information
- Remember details and follow steps to complete a task
- Hold on to information while considering other information
- Identify and propose cause-and-effect relationships
- Cluster and arrange information into categories

11. *Gathering data with all senses* means paying attention to the world around you. Gathering data through all the senses: sight, sound, smell, taste, and touch. We know that all information gets into the brain through the sensory pathways. Many scientists say we have nine senses: External senses that are engaged from external sources include sight, sound, taste, touch, and smell. They provide information about the outside world. Pain, balance, thirst, and hunger are considered to be our internal senses. They provide information about the body and its needs.

Most linguistic, cultural, and physical learning is derived from the environment by observing or taking it in through the senses. To know an apple, it must be eaten; to know a role, it must be acted; to know a game, it must be played; to know a dance, it must be moved.

When something is learned or practiced using a variety of different senses, there is duplication of that memory stored in multiple parts of the brain. For example, when our memory is activated, like remembering a painting at a museum, other memories, like whether the room was hot, cold, or smelly, are almost immediately co-activated. This means that the more senses through which information is experienced, the more places in our memory the information will be stored and the more likely it will be remembered. Multi-sensory storage not only provides better access to retrieve the information, it also provides multiple brain pathways to activate the information for new applications, to solve new problems, and for creative innovations.

12. *Creating, imagining, and innovating* means generating possibilities; playing with new ideas. Creativity is thought of by many psychologists to be the highest order of thinking. Creativity is the act of turning new and imaginative ideas into reality and is characterized by the ability to perceive the world in new ways, to find hidden patterns, to make connections between seemingly unrelated phenomena, and to generate solutions, insights, or ideas. Creativity involves two processes: thinking, then producing (Naiman, 2021).

Human beings have the capacity to generate novel, original, clever or ingenious products, solutions, and techniques—if that capacity is developed. Creativity and imagination are the most sought-after dispositions because they enrich our understanding and can make life more pleasurable. Creativity starts with imagination, and history shows that what can be imagined can actually be created.

Creative human beings try to conceive solutions differently, examining alternative possibilities from many angles. They tend to project themselves into different roles using analogies, starting with a vision and working backward or imagining they are the objects being considered. Creative people take risks and frequently push the boundaries of their perceived limits (Perkins, 1985). They are often intrinsically rather than extrinsically motivated, working on a task because of the aesthetic challenge rather than the material rewards. Creative people hold up their products for others to judge and seek feedback in an ever-increasing effort to refine their technique.

13. *Taking responsible risks* means being adventuresome; living on the edge of your competence. *Risk* may be defined as undertaking a task in which there is a lack of certainty or a fear of failure. Risk takers seem to have an almost uncontrollable urge to go beyond established limits. However, all risks are not worth taking. When taking a *responsible* risk, they take into account what their past experience has taught them. Yet, they are uneasy about too much comfort; they "live on the edge of their competence." They seem compelled to place themselves in situations where they do not know what the outcome will be. They accept complexity, confusion, uncertainty, and the higher risks of failure as part of their normal process and they learn to view setbacks as interesting, challenging, and growth producing.

Some learners seem reluctant to take risks. They may be fearful about the consequences of failure and feel it more prudent to continue doing what they have always done. They hold back in games, new learning, and new friendships because their fear of failure is far greater than their sense of venture or adventure. Their inner voice may say, "if you don't try it, you won't be wrong" or "if you try it and you are wrong, you will look stupid." When someone is averse to taking risks, however, they are confronted constantly with missed opportunities. They miss hearing another inner voice that might say, "if you don't try it, you will never know." They become trapped in fear and mistrust that they might be wrong or that what they are considering won't work. They are unable to sustain a process of problem-solving and finding the answer over time, and therefore avoid ambiguous situations. They have a need for certainty rather than an inclination for doubt.

Responsible risk-takers draw on past knowledge, are mindful of options, thoughtful about consequences, and have a well-trained sense of what is appropriate. They know that some risks are worth taking.

14. *Finding humor* means searching for the whimsical, incongruous, and unexpected. Being able to laugh at yourself. Another unique attribute of humans is our sense of humor. We all laugh! Its positive effects on psychological functions include a drop in the pulse rate, the secretion of endorphins, and increased oxygen in the blood. It has been found to liberate creativity and provoke such higher-level thinking skills as anticipation, finding novel relationships, visual imagery, and making analogies.

Some people find humor in all the "wrong" places—human differences, ineptitude, injurious behavior, vulgarity, violence, and profanity. Laughing *at* is jeering and ridicule, targeting outsiders who look or act differently, or driving them away. They laugh at others yet are unable to laugh at themselves. Being laughed at can lead to bullying and violence. Inappropriate use of humor creates tension rather than providing a release of tension.

When people are laughing *with* one another, they experience the pleasure of acceptance, and they bond with one another. People who find humor perceive situations from original and often interesting vantage points. They tend to initiate humor more often, to place greater value on finding humor, to appreciate and understand others' humor, and to be verbally playful when interacting with others. Having a whimsical frame of mind, they thrive on finding incongruity and perceiving absurdities, ironies, and satire; they find discontinuities and are able to laugh at situations and themselves (Provine, 2012). Thoughtful people can distinguish between situations of human frailty and fallibility, which are in need of compassion, and those that are truly funny (Dyer, 1997).

15. *Responding with wonderment and awe* means finding the world awesome, mysterious, and being intrigued with phenomena and beauty. Wonderment and awe are the feelings we have when we recognize that something is amazing. Wanting to experience these feelings is what makes us strive to achieve great things, to set and work toward BIG goals. Wonderment fills us with a sense of fascination about mysteries yet unsolved or questions yet unanswered. It leaves us with renewed appreciation of the ordinary things before us.

Efficacious thinkers have a passion for what they do. They have not only an "*I can*" attitude, but also an "*I enjoy*" feeling. They seek problems to solve for themselves and to submit to others. They delight in discovering new ideas, making up problems to solve, and enjoying the enigmas that others present.

They find the incredible in the everyday objects often taken for granted. They are curious—they commune with the world around them, pause to reflect on the changing formations of a cloud, feel charmed by the opening of a bud, sense the logical simplicity of mathematical order, and allow the amazing parts of life to inspire them. They find beauty in a sunset, intrigue in the geometrics of a spider web, and exhilarate at the iridescence of a hummingbird's wings. They see the congruity and intricacies in the derivation of a mathematical formula, recognize the orderliness and adroitness of a chemical change, and commune with the serenity of a distant constellation. They feel compelled, enthusiastic, and passionate about learning, inquiring, and mastering. They recognize and celebrate the beauty and wonder of the universe and let their minds be intrigued by the mystery of the things they cannot yet understand. Responding with wonderment and awe is the habit that makes us ask big questions, that inspires us to achieve great things.

16. *Remaining open to continuous learning* means having humility and admitting when you don't know and are curious to find out. Learning throughout your lifetime. The human brain can continue to develop throughout one's lifetime. Efficacious people are in a continuous learning mode. Their confidence, in combination with their inquisitiveness, allows them to constantly search for new and better ways. They are always striving for improvement, always growing, always learning, always modifying, and improving themselves. They seize problems, situations, tensions, conflicts, and circumstances as valuable opportunities to learn.

A great mystery about some humans is that they confront learning opportunities with fear rather than mystery and wonder. They are content with what they already believe and know. They seem to feel better when they know rather than when they learn. They defend their biases, beliefs, and storehouses of knowledge rather than inviting the unknown, the creative, and the inspirational. Being certain and closed gives them comfort while being doubtful and open gives them fear.

From an early age, students are trained to believe that deep learning means figuring out the "right answer," rather than developing capabilities for effective and thoughtful action. They have been taught to value certainty rather than doubt, to give answers rather than to inquire, to know which choice is correct rather than to explore alternatives.

Efficacious humans are eager to learn. That includes the humility of knowing what we don't know, which is the highest form of thinking we will ever learn. Paradoxically, unless we start off with humility we will never get anywhere, so the first step will eventually be the crowning glory of all learning: the humility to know—and admit—that we don't know, and not be afraid to find out (Bateson, 2005).

SUMMARY

Although we separated each habit for the purpose of teaching, there are many that work as clusters. For example, when persisting, it helps to consider other alternatives by thinking flexibly. When listening to someone with understanding and empathy, you will also have to manage your impulsivity. Many schools decide how to organize teaching the habits. For example, some teachers like to choose one a month. What is most important is that the students learn (1) what the meaning of the habit is, (2) what strategies they might use to strengthen the habit, and (3) have the opportunity to reflect on what they are discovering about themselves as effective thinkers and problem solvers.

People who internalize the Habits of Mind expand their personal power. They are more likely to have a broader view of what is possible. They may ask themselves, "What strategies do I have at my disposal that could benefit others?" "How might I use this opportunity to reaffirm my continuing quest for a world that is filled with justice, dignity, and love?" The future depends on people who have dedicated themselves to solving problems the answers to which are not yet apparent. When we internalize the Habits of Mind, we strengthen our capacity to know what to do when we don't know what to do. The ultimate outcomes of internalizing the Habits of Mind are optimism, confidence, and hope.

REFERENCES

Asmus, M. J. (2017). The neuroscience of asking insightful questions. *Government Executive*. Retrieved from www.govexec.com/management/2017/04/neuroscience-asking-insightful-questions/137274.

Bateson, M. C. (2005). Learning is key to bridging the intergenerational gap. *Leverage Points*, 64. Pegasus Communications, Inc.

Costa, A., & Kallick, B. (2008). *Learning and leading with Habits of Mind: 16 characteristics for success.* Alexandria, VA: Association for Supervision and Curriculum Development.

Dyer, J. (1997). Humor as process. In A. Costa & R. Liebmann (Eds.), *Envisioning process as content: Toward a renaissance curriculum* (pp. 211–229). Thousand Oaks, CA: Corwin Press.

Edwards, J. (2014). *Habits of mind: A synthesis of the research.* Institute for Habits of Mind. Retrieved from https://www.habitsofmindinstitute.org/shop/research-habits-mind-2/

Feuerstein, R., Rand, Y. M., Hoffman, M. B., & Miller, R. (1980). *Instrumental enrichment: An intervention program for cognitive modifiability.* Baltimore: University Park Press.

Lieberman, Daniel. (2016). http://www.uctv.tv/ daniel lieberman youtube.

Naiman, L. (2021). What is creativity? (And why is it a crucial factor for business success?). *Creativity at Work.* Retrieved from www.creativityatwork.com.

Perkins, D. (1985). What creative thinking is. In A. L. Costa (Ed.), *Developing minds: A resource book for teaching thinking* (pp. 85–88). Alexandria, VA: Association for Supervision and Curriculum Development.

Provine, R. (2012). Beyond a joke: The truth about why we laugh. *The Observer*, September. Retrieved from www.theguardian.com/books/2012/sep/02/why-we-laugh-psychology-provine.

Schwab, K. (2016). The Fourth Industrial Revolution. World Economic Forum. Retrieved from https://www.weforum.org/about/the-fourth-industrial-revolution-by-klaus-schwab

Chapter 2

Mindful and Thoughtful Dispositions as Habits of Mind

Servet Altan

Similar to how the work and responsibilities of a conductor may be underappreciated, many people perceive that teaching is an easy job. They may not appreciate how teachers need to be aware of the learning needs of all their students and to conduct their class in such a way that all learners are involved. Furthermore, with today's rigorous performance standards and high stakes testing, and changing paradigms teaching is becoming even more complicated and demanding. That is why we, as educators, need to have mindful and thoughtful Habits of Mind more than ever.

The importance of thoughtfulness and mindfulness to make professional conduct more intelligent was mentioned earlier by Dottin (2009). *Mindfulness* (supportive of learning) and *thoughtfulness* (directly related to learning) help to ground pedagogical dispositions as habits of pedagogical mindfulness and thoughtfulness that render professional actions and conduct more intelligent. Mindfulness and thoughtfulness are key factors in acting intelligently, for to get results without intelligent control of means is to forego intelligent inquiry and intelligently controlled habit.

DISPOSITIONS AS 16 HABITS OF MIND

Although viewing dispositions as clusters of habits is not a new idea, using Costa and Kallick's model of 16 Habits of Mind to explore teachers' dispositions is rarely mentioned in the literature. Costa and Kallick's 16 Habits of Mind are offered as mindful and thoughtful dispositions toward behaving intelligently when confronted with a problem to which the answer is not known (Costa & Kallick, 2008, pp. xx–xxi). Each Habit of Mind includes intelligent behaviors that are expected to be in action when a specific disposition is displayed.

Intelligent behaviors are the external outcomes of the interaction between our cognition and emotions; they are what we can observe unlike neurological processes (Perez-Alvarez & Timoneda-Gallart, 2007). These behaviors may provide clues about one's cognitive processes and functioning, skills, strategies, and one's disposition. For example, if a person has the Habit to Think Flexibly, that person displays the intelligent behavior of changing perspective and generates alternatives as well as considering a variety of options.

Sometimes these behaviors are self-evident and observable, but in other cases one needs to inquire into these behaviors as they may include cognitive processes that are not directly observable. In the following sections, Habits of Mind are discussed in relation to learning theories that are supportive of learning (*Mindfulness*) and directive to learning (*Thoughtfulness*). Educators can use the findings of research from established theories to help their students develop desired Habits of Mind.[1]

MINDFULNESS AND HABITS OF MIND

The increasingly complex dynamics of schools as learning environments demands teachers to possess the habits of mind to be able to pertain and develop their emotional and psychological well-being when faced with problems. Teachers may face many challenges during a school day and then continue teaching while trying to contribute to students' emotional and psychological well-being. Several Habits of Mind include intelligent behaviors that have affective attributes. The theories of mindfulness and emotional intelligence serve to further understand these behaviors.

Mindfulness Theory and Habits of Mind

Schools as being one of the most dynamic working places teachers may face many challenges during a school day which can affect teachers' psychological well-being, and thus the supportive classroom environment. Mindfulness practices can contribute to emotional self-regulation and improve flexibility of teachers and students. Integrating mindfulness practice into education can increase teachers' psychological well-being and contribute to positive relationships between teachers and students (Meiklejohn et al., 2012).

Several theorists and researchers have explained what is meant by mindfulness. Kabat-Zinn (2003) defines mindfulness as paying attention on purpose, being in the present moment, and non-judgmentally . . . unfolding the experience moment by moment. The idea is for individuals to be aware and conscious of their thinking processes. Langer (2000) defined mindfulness as a flexible state of mind in which we are actively engaged in the present, noticing new things and sensitive to context.

Hoyt (2016) defines mindfulness as the energy of attention. It is the capacity in each of us to be present one hundred percent to what is happening within and around us. It is the miracle that allows us to become fully alive in each moment. All three definitions hold implications for the benefits of practicing mindfulness in educational settings such as thinking before acting, giving thinking time for students before they rush in for the answers and solutions, and paying full attention.

Mindfulness is relatively new to K-12 education; however, teacher professional programs in many countries offer mindfulness training. Roeser et al. (2012) have created Mindfulness Training programs for teachers to develop habits of mind related to awareness of one's thinking processes. They suggest that helping teachers be more mindful improves their health and well-being; they learn how to create positive learning environments for their students.

Sustained and structured mindfulness programs fundamental for educators to support learners' cognitive skills for learning and their capacity for distress tolerance. As schools are places where students spend most of their times, in-school mindfulness practices may help students enhance their emotional competence and manage negative emotions. Through sustained and structured mindfulness programs (e.g., learning2breathe.org) may help reduce negative feelings and increase calmness and relaxation (Broderick & Metz, 2009).

Mindfulness practices can also help students become more aware of their own feelings and manage negative emotions. Therefore, educators should be knowledgeable about cognitive and emotional developmental processes. Findings from Mindfulness research and related intelligent behaviors can provide strategies to support the development of teachers' mindful intelligent behaviors associated with Habits of Mind.

These Habits of Mind are: gathering data through all senses, managing impulsivity, responding with wonderment and awe, and taking responsible risks. The intelligent behaviors that are associated with these Habits of Mind are: being aware of the pathways for gathering data and making use of a variety of sources; paying attention to the world around; taking time and thinking before acting; remaining calm, thoughtful, and reflective; accepting confusion, uncertainty, and the higher risks of failure as part of the normal process, and not behaving impulsively.

Emotional Intelligence and Intelligent Behaviors
Associated with Habits of Mind

Emotions can direct our short and long-term thoughts (Ritchhart, 2001). When we encounter a situation that we can feel empathy for, then our emotions may guide us to do something about that situation. The increasing number of demands and stressors teachers face can influence their ways of thinking and their ability to manage emotions. Therefore, K-12 teachers and teacher educators need to address emotion in education more explicitly to help their students improve their social and emotional competence.

Emotions cannot be separated from learning (Ferro, 1993). Teachers' social and emotional competence and well-being affect the classroom climate and students' social and emotional and academic outcomes. Emotional Intelligence includes the abilities to accurately perceive emotions, to access and generate emotions to assist thought, to understand emotions and emotional knowledge, and to reflectively regulate emotions to promote emotional and intellectual growth (Mayer, Caruso, & Salovey, 2004).

Teachers and teacher educators can use intelligent behaviors to identify strategies that help their students and pre-service teachers become socially and emotionally more competent. For instance, they can place value on a sense of humor and how it may contribute to supportive learning environments. Likewise, they can model these behaviors by gently attending to another person or remaining calm and not behaving impulsively

THOUGHTFULNESS AND HABITS OF MIND

Teaching is a reflective practice that renders the union of thoughts and feelings. Pedagogical thoughtfulness has long been discussed as one of the concepts that is basis for effective teaching and learning. In this sense, *thoughtfulness* refers to being mindful of one's thinking processes and reflecting on experiences. Through reflective practices, one can construct new knowledge (Constructivism) and regulate learning strategies and motivation (Self-Regulated Learning Theory). Therefore, Habits of Mind that are related to thoughtfulness associated with learning theories that are directive to learning.

Constructivism and Habits of Mind

So far many educational theorists have supported that learners construct knowledge. For Piaget (1994) acquisition of knowledge is a life-long process through which we re-structure and modify our experiences based on the existing schemes in our minds to expand these existing schemes to accommodate the new knowledge or situation. Therefore, learning becomes meaningful only if the new knowledge is relevant to the existing schemes.

In constructivism there is an emphasis on modeling new behaviors through careful observation, working in teams, building upon prior experience and knowledge, transferring the prior knowledge to novel situations, questioning and inquiring, collaborating with others and use of language as a means of communication, and gathering data using a variety of sources especially sources from real life (Bandura, 1977). The importance of the application of past knowledge to new situations, cooperative learning, developing, and using mental maps, inquiring, and clarity in communication are consistent with Habits of Mind.

Incremental Theory, Growth Mindset, and Habits of Mind

Mindsets can shape social success at school as well as academic success and this is promising for educators and parents. There has been a growing body of research demonstrating that growth mindset behaviors can help thwart depression and aggression and help increase power and creativity. Since intellectual ability beliefs have roots in parenting and education, this means it is important to appreciate that a fixed mindset can be reset (Dweck, 2016).

Research has shown that positive attitudes and perceptions about learning are key for successful learning and that both teacher and student motivation may affect student achievement (Haimovitz et al., 2011). Successful learners constantly look for ways to improve and see challenges as opportunities to learn, they have high expectations of themselves, they are eager to learn throughout their lives, and they strive for improvement, growing, learning, and improving themselves.

Self-Regulated Learning Theory and Habits of Mind

In an era of technological distractions, self-regulated learning is becoming more important. Self-regulation implies learners monitor and govern their own learning. They resist being distracted and reactive to external motivations. It involves understanding and controlling learning environments. The ability for self-regulation can be a predictor of students' success in school as learners find a way to succeed even in the cases of obstacles, poor study conditions, demotivating teachers, or unclear texts (Zimmerman, 2002).

Self-regulated learning strategies can be learned from instruction and modeling by parents, teachers, coaches, and peers. In fact, self-regulated learners seek out help from others to improve their learning. Teachers can model strategies to monitor one's learning. Children learn to regulate thoughts, feeling, behavior, and emotion by watching and responding to adults' self-regulation (Florez, 2011). For example, teachers can show their students how planning results in positive outcomes and reduces anxiety.

Teachers can also model persisting in complex situations and not giving up as persisting through challenging tasks can help learners regulate their anxiety and teachers can show how they persist in the face of challenges. These strategies may help individuals understand and control their learning environment and help them plan, monitor, and evaluate their own learning. In other words, they will develop ways of thinking that help them regulate and monitor their own learning. Individuals can improve their self-regulatory processes by setting goals and selecting appropriate strategies to achieve their purposes.

SUMMARY

Since the pedagogical Mindfulness (*supportive of learning*) and Thoughtfulness (*directly related to learning*) clusters are related to established theories as a result of the comprehensive conceptual framework developed by Altan, Lane, and Dottin (2019), teachers can use the findings from empirical research associated with those theories to guide their students' development of intelligent behaviors and Habits of Mind. For example, research that supports Constructivism can be used to develop the Habit of Applying Past Knowledge to New Situations. The associated intelligent behaviors can be observed to learn how the disposition is being developed.

Likewise, research that supports Incremental Theory can be used to develop the Habit of Remaining Open to Continuous Learning. Students who have this Habit of Mind will exhibit behaviors such as continuously searching for new and better ways and striving for improvement, growing, learning, modifying, and improving themselves. In another case, the educator might need to develop students' Habit of Metacognition. In this case, educators can investigate Self-Regulated Learning Theory to help students develop intelligent behaviors such as developing an action plan and being aware of one's own thoughts and their effects on others.

Another situation might occur when a methods teacher notices that a student overreacts to challenges and conflicts. The educator might also be concerned that the student makes quick judgments and is not reflective. This educator could research Mindfulness Theory to identify strategies to develop mindful behaviors associated with the Habit of Managing Impulsivity. A similar situation can be when an educator might be concerned that students are not sensitive to the needs of others. Then, the educator could research into

Emotional Intelligence theory to help students develop the Habit of Thinking Interdependently.

Each of the 16 habits proposed by Costa and Kallick could be addressed in this fashion and educators can benefit from using the conceptual framework to better understand their students' dispositions and help them develop mindful and thoughtful intelligent behaviors.

NOTE

1. Original article previously published by Altan, Lane, and Dottin in *Journal of Teacher Education*, 2019.

REFERENCES

Altan, S., Lane, J. F., & Dottin, E. (2019). Using habits of mind, intelligent behaviors, and educational theories to create a conceptual framework for developing effective teaching dispositions. *Journal of Teacher Education, 70*(2), 169–183.

Bandura, A. (1977). *Social learning theory.* Englewood Cliffs, NJ: Prentice-Hall.

Broderick, P. C., & Metz, S. (2009). Learning to BREATHE: A pilot trial of a mindfulness curriculum for adolescents. *Advances in School Mental Health Promotion, 2,* 35–46.

Costa, A. L., & Kallick, B. (2008). *Learning and leading with habits of mind: 16 essential characteristics for success.* Alexandria, VA: ASCD.

Darling-Hammond, L., & Bransford, J. (with LePage, P., Hammerness, K., & Duffy, H.). (2005). *Preparing teachers for a changing world: What teachers should learn and be able to do.* San Francisco: Jossey-Bass.

Dottin, E. (2009). Professional judgment and dispositions in teacher education. *Teaching and Teacher Education, 25,* 83–88.

Dweck, C. S. (2016). The remarkable reach of growth mind-sets. *Scientific American Mind, 27*(1), 36–41.

Ferro, R. T. (1993). The influence of affective processing in education and training. *New Directions for Adult and Continuing Education, 59,* 25–33.

Florez, R. I. (2011). Developing young children's self-regulation through everyday experiences. *Young Children,* 46–51.

Haimovitz, K., Wormington, S. V., & Corpus, J. H. (2011). Dangerous mindsets: How beliefs about intelligence predict motivational change. *Learning and Individual Differences, 21,* 747–752.

Hoyt, M. (2016). Teaching with mindfulness: The pedagogy of being-with/for and without being-with/for. *Journal of Curriculum Theorizing, 31*(1), 126–142.

Kabat-Zinn, J. (2003). Mindfulness-based interventions in context: past, present, and future. *Clinical Psychology: Science & Practice, 10*(2), 144–156.

Langer, E. J. (2000). Mindful learning. *Current Directions in Psychological Science,* *9*(6), 220–223.

Mayer, J. D., Caruso, D. R., & Salovey, P. (2004). Emotional intelligence: Theory, findings and implications. *Psychological Inquiry, 60,* 197–215.

Meiklejohn, J., Phillips, C., Freedman, M. L., Griffin, M. L., Biegel, G., Roach, A., . . . Saltzman, A. (2012). Integrating mindfulness training into K-12 education: Fostering the resilience of teachers and students. *Mindfulness, 3*(4), 291–307.

Perez-Alvarez, F., & Timoneda-Gallart, C. (2007). *A better look at intelligent behavior; cognition and emotion.* New York: Nova Science Publishers.

Piaget, J. (1994). Cognitive development in children: Piaget development and learning. *Journal of Research in Science Teaching, 2,* 176–186.

Ritchhart, R. (2001). From IQ to IC: A dispositional view of intelligence. *Roeper Review, 23*(3), 143–150.

Roeser, R. W., Skinner, E. A., Beers, J., & Jennings, P. A. (2012). Mindfulness training and teachers' professional development: An emerging area of research and practice. *Child Development Perspectives, 6,* 146–153.

Zimmerman, B. J. (2002). Becoming a self-regulated learner: An overview. *Theory into Practice, 41,* 64–72.

Chapter 3

Research on the Habits of Mind

Jennifer L. Edwards

Numerous researchers have investigated the 16 Habits of Mind (HoM) (Costa & Kallick, 2000) in a variety of contexts. This chapter includes information about studies with elementary, secondary, and postsecondary students. It also contains studies with teachers, superintendents, and prison inmates. In addition, this chapter has a section in which researchers positioned the HoM in other bodies of literature. It concludes with a summary.

Studies were chosen because they contributed to the understanding of Habits of Mind and were published in journals, dissertations, or theses with two exceptions. The exceptions were included because they provided important contributions to the field. Studies showing the efficacy of the Habits of Mind were also chosen because they focused on at least eight of the Habits of Mind. Earlier studies appear first in each section and are followed by later studies in chronological order.

STUDIES WITH STUDENTS

A number of researchers have investigated the HoM (Costa & Kallick, 2000) with students. This section contains information about studies with elementary students, secondary students, and postsecondary students.

Elementary Students

Five researchers have studied the HoM in elementary schools. They include Matsuoka (2007), Tabor et al. (2008), Burgess (2012), Royce (2015), and Teeple (2021).

In a longitudinal study, Matsuoka (2007) followed students who learned the HoM and participated in the Philosophy for Children Hawai'i in elementary school to determine whether their learnings would carry over into middle school. She conducted focus groups, the students wrote in journals, and she conducted follow-up interviews. She also interviewed their parents and their teachers. "When faced with difficult choices or situations, these students used Habits of the Mind and Philosophy for Children Hawai'i to think critically, solve problems, and make informed decisions" (pp. 259–260).

Tabor et al. (2008) conducted a study at Waikiki Elementary School when it had used the HoM for more than 20 years. Students, faculty members, and people in the community had created a culture around the Habits of Mind by implementing it into their daily lives. According to Tabor et al., "this school culture results in a dynamic learning community in which all participants are challenged to become ever more mindful, ever more thoughtful learners to support the collective efforts of the school" (p. 360).

The students at Waikiki Elementary School came from difficult backgrounds, including 40 percent of the students living in homes with a single parent and 40 percent of the students getting free and reduced lunches (Tabor et al., 2008). Waikiki advanced to become a Blue Ribbon School by 1995 and a National Blue Ribbon recipient in 2007. In a survey of Hawaii's best schools in *Honolulu Magazine's* May 2008 issue, Waikiki School was given an A+ based on test scores and desirability, and was ranked fifth of 258 schools (p. 350).

Burgess (2012) investigated the impact of teaching 8 of the 16 HoM to 15 children from age 7 to 12 in Australian schools. She surveyed and interviewed the children, their parents, and their teachers both before the intervention and after it. She found that their "problematic behaviors" decreased (p. 47). The students increased in all of the HoM. They "believed they were becoming more accepted by their peers and also felt that they were 'in trouble' less with adults" (p. 58).

Royce (2015) studied the HoM character education program in an elementary school during the 2008–2009 school year to determine its effectiveness in increasing student achievement and helping students to engage in behaviors that were appropriate in schools. Royce found that students attending third and fourth grade improved in their academic performance, and students from kindergarten through third grade showed improved behavior. Royce suggested that the school continue with the program, include parents and other support people in training, continue training teachers, and recognize what teachers are doing to teach the HoM.

Teeple (2021) studied 17 students in the fifth grade as well as 3 teachers to determine the relationship between the HoM and student social presence and performance in online learning. Twelve students participated in Group

1 and had high ratings on the Habits of Mind by themselves, their parents, and their teacher. Five students participated in Group 2 and had low ratings on the HoM.

Students were asked to rate themselves on a variety of aspects of social presence in the online environment (Teeple, 2021). Students who were more proficient in the HoM had higher summative writing scores, and they believed that persistence made them successful. Regarding the Habits of Mind that appeared most evident in efficacious student work habits, both student and teacher interview responses frequently cited Persistence, Thinking Flexibly, Thinking About Your Thinking (Metacognition), Striving for Accuracy, and Thinking and Communicating with Clarity and Precision (p. 64).

Secondary Students

Seven studies have been conducted on the HoM at the secondary level. They include Marshall (2004), Chang et al. (2011), Bee et al. (2013), Shaeffer et al. (2014), Margeson (2018), Muscott (2018), and Vazquez (2020).

Marshall (2004) studied 16 students who were taking a precalculus course while receiving instruction in the HoM for 5 months. Students wrote in journals, took surveys before and after the intervention, and participated in focus groups. They grew from pretest to posttest on 9 of the 12 HoM on which their instructor had focused, although not significantly. Students indicated that the HoM would help them in the areas of "jobs, efficiency in school work, setting goals, having a good future, being a better worker, making others happy, respecting others, and being a better person" (p. 38).

Chang et al. (2011) administered the 75-item Habits of Mind Inventory to students at Kailua High School to discover how the HoM might be related to risk of violence, whether students would succeed in academic endeavors, and how often they would be suspended. "All except questioning/problem solving and taking responsible risks were significantly and negatively associated with violence risk. . . . The more risk factors a student had, the lower their GPA and greater likelihood that they were suspended. . . . Persisting was consistently associated with higher GPA and fewer suspensions" (pp. 4–5).

Bee et al. (2013) studied six 12-year-old children in Malaysia. They were participating in an English as a Second Language (ESL) class and had been learning English for five years. In the study, they read silently and then chose a pre-written question to answer. Next, they discussed the answers. Bee et al. recorded their conversations to determine which of the HoM the students used. In their discussions, the students used nearly all of the HoM. "The students were seen rereading the texts, pausing to think at intervals, attempting to state their points clearly, seeking clarification and trying to find the best answer to the questions posed" (p. 132).

Bee et al. (2013) observed the students using the HoM 650 times. They most frequently used the Habits of Mind of Questioning and Posing Problems, Thinking and Communicating with Clarity and Precision, and Applying Past Knowledge to New Situations. The researchers also noticed patterns; for example, when students asked questions, they had to apply prior knowledge to new situations. They also needed to think and communicate with clarity and precision, and they were required to listen with understanding and empathy to each other.

Shaeffer et al. (2014) conducted a study of three science teachers at the high school level who taught the HoM of Persistence and Thinking Interdependently for four weeks. Although they just taught the two Habits of Mind, they exposed their students to eight of the Habits of Mind and assessed them. The students measured the HoM with a rubric they had created, were observed, wrote in journals about the two HoM in which they felt the strongest and the two in which they wanted to improve, created a video of a HoM, and participated in an interview at the end of the study.

Shaeffer et al. (2014) wanted to discover "whether explicit instruction in the HoM would increase metacognition, improve collaboration and develop other traits that have proven necessary for success in school and in life" (p. 2). The students grew in the two HoM for which they received instruction. In contrast, they decreased in the other HoM. The researchers suggested that the students might have been judging themselves more critically as a result of becoming more aware of the HoM.

Margeson (2018) investigated the perceptions of 10 teachers who taught ninth grade about the HoM and the academic success of students. The teachers focused on the HoM of Thinking Flexibly, Applying Past Knowledge to New Situations, Managing Impulsivity, Remaining Open to Continuous Learning, and Persistence. Margeson found that "teachers perceived habits of mind as necessary for success, handling adversity, and adapting to life beyond high school" (Abstract).

Muscott (2018) examined data from 354 middle school students in social studies classes and 246 high schools in English Language Arts to determine whether a relationship existed between their use of the HoM and their scores on performance assessments. He used multiple linear regression to compare student achievement on performance assessments and their achievement in the HoM when compared with their acquisition of knowledge and their ability to understand "the big conceptual ideas of a unit" (p. 3). The correlation was stronger for middle school students taking social studies than for high school students taking English Language Arts.

Vazquez (2020) gathered data from eight teachers who taught high school juniors and eight students who were in the junior class and had started receiving instruction in the HoM in the eighth grade. The participants engaged in focus groups and interviews. The students also submitted work samples. The purpose of the study was to determine the participants' perceptions of how instruction in the HoM had impacted the students.

Vazquez (2020) concluded that the HoM provide a common language for teachers and students to use. They also help students to think critically and engage in solving problems. The HoM enable students to gain knowledge, and the HoM help students to be successful after they graduate from high school. "They identified the teaching of Habits of Mind as valuable; needed for critical, creative thinking and problem solving; needed for academic and social success; and for success in life" (p. 221).

Postsecondary Students

One study has been conducted with postsecondary students. Hill (2021) studied an initiative called Honoring Adult Behaviors and Influencing Thinking Skills (HABITS) in the Frances County Adult Education (FCAE) system. It included the HoM and Integrated Educational Training. She investigated the benefits students wanted to obtain from participating in the program along with their satisfaction with the program. The study ran for four months. Out of 343 students who were enrolled in the program, she gathered quantitative data from 189 participants, and she conducted interviews with 12 participants.

Hill (2021) found that the students were committed to themselves and wanted to improve. They wanted to be able to have access to more education at a later time, and they wanted to have a better life. The HABITS program was "a value-added component" and contributed to the students being satisfied (p. v). She suggested that FCAE should be "pursing student satisfaction as a programmatic goal; engaging in behaviors that foster trust; offering thinking habits as a foundational practice; and working to ensure high quality workforce-related training opportunities for participants" (pp. v–vi).

STUDIES WITH TEACHERS

Two studies have been done on the HoM with teachers. The researchers included Owens (2012) and Altan and Lane (2018).

Owens (2012) conducted a 6-year study in two schools in which he explored the processes the teachers used in their Professional Learning Communities (PLCs) while implementing the HoM in their classrooms. He found that such an initiative requires everyone in the school to commit to the work. He also discovered that when teachers used the language of the HoM in the PLCs, they were able to "build a sense of collective vision and mission through the establishment of shared understandings. . . . while also supporting the development of a highly thoughtful, supportive and collaborative culture within the school communities" (p. 274).

Altan and Lane (2018) interviewed five teachers in Turkey who had been highly rated on the 16 HoM to discover the life experiences that had contributed to their excellence in these areas. They found that Learning Environments and Personal Attributes contributed to the teachers having high levels of the HoM. The teachers reported that they were raised with parents who were "supportive, permissive, responsive, and democratic" (p. 243). "Their parents, while being kind and caring, had firm rules and high expectations" (pp. 243–244). Their parents looked at things positively, had a high value for education, and enjoyed humor.

Altan and Lane (2018) suggested that *"Learning Environments* may contribute to . . . finding humor, listening with understanding and empathy, managing impulsivity, remaining open to continuous learning, responding with wonderment and awe, persisting, thinking flexibly, and thinking interdependently" (p. 245, italics in original). Teachers said they enjoyed "reading, travelling, having hobbies, and spending time in nature" (p. 245). The researchers connected these with "listening with understanding and empathy, remaining open to continuous learning, responding with wonderment and awe, striving for accuracy, thinking flexibly" (p. 245).

Travelling helped the teachers to have more empathy with their students who came from other cultures (Altan & Lane, 2018). Reading enabled the teachers to be powerful role models for their students. The time the teachers spent in nature enabled them to have peace, and the teachers' hobbies helped them to increase in creativity. The researchers suggested that those who provide teacher education programs could benefit from incorporating the results of this study into their work with pre-service teachers as well as in-service teachers.

A STUDY WITH SUPERINTENDENTS

One study has been conducted with school superintendents. Harper (2020) studied three superintendents to determine the HoM they used "that contribute[d] to their leading schools in making significant improvements in academic performance for all while reducing achievement gaps" (p. 72). Harper interviewed them, administered the Habits of Mind Self-Assessment survey, reviewed documents, took field notes, and observed them. In addition to gathering data from the superintendents, he gathered data from approximately 10 people who worked with each of them.

The superintendents all practiced the same five HoM (Harper, 2020). They were:

1. Managing Impulsivity
2. Persistence
3. Taking Responsible Risks
4. Creating, Imagining, Innovating
5. Remaining Open to Continuous Learning (p. 216)

Harper (2020) concluded that "this core set of Habits of Mind are important skills, attributes and or dispositions successful school leaders need to effectively problem-solve the complex issues of improving the outcomes of all students" (p. 216). Furthermore, he suggested that professionals can learn the skills.

A STUDY WITH PRISON INMATES

One study has been conducted with prison inmates. Houston (2009) and Workforce Development Partnership (2013) discussed the initiative of the Community High School of Vermont to use the HoM and place inmates in businesses over a 3-year period. Prison inmates learned the Habits of Mind and had the opportunity to use the skills immediately. The security officers used the language of HoM with the inmates, and the inmates referred to the HoM as "my Habits of Mind" (p. 5).

As a result of being trained in HoM, participants were more likely to stay out of prison (Houston, 2009). Ninety-one percent of the men in the experimental group obtained employment within 30 days of release, versus 64 percent of the control group. Using 6 months in the labor force as the measure of employment retention, the analysis found that 95 percent of the men who obtained employment retained it, versus 64 percent for the control group (pp. 6–7).

Staff also received training in the HoM (Houston, 2009; Workforce Development Partnership, 2013). They were more satisfied with their job and felt more positively toward what they were doing. They also reported that they were able to communicate more effectively with the inmates and with those with whom they worked.

THE RELATIONSHIP OF THE HABITS OF MIND
WITH LITERATURE IN OTHER AREAS

Three related studies have been published on the HoM (Alexander & Vermette, 2019; Alhamlan et al., 2018; Altan et al., 2019). The researchers compared the HoM with literature in other areas.

Alhamlan et al. (2018) conducted a systematic review and meta-analysis to determine how the habits of mind in the Framework for Success in Postsecondary Writing (O'Neill et al., 2012) were related to "the development of critical thinking" (p. 25). The Framework contained habits of mind that overlapped with the HoM proposed by Costa and Kallick (2000).

Alhamlan et al. (2018) used multiple regression with "five independent variables as predictors (gathering all data through senses, thinking flexibly, persisting, thinking and communicating with clarity and precision, and metacognition) and the critical thinking rate as a dependent variable" (p. 30). They found that "habits of mind are related to the development of critical thinking skills, while its effect is varying from one habit to another and requires n-depth [*sic*] investigation for multiple disciplines" (p. 33).

Alexander and Vermette (2019) demonstrated how the HoM overlap with the Collaborative for Academic, Social, and Emotional Learning (CASEL, 2018) competencies. They suggested that first CASEL competency, "self-awareness," overlaps with the HoM of "metacognition" and "remaining open to continuous learning" (p. 5). They believed that the second CASEL competency, "self-management," overlaps with "managing impulsivity," "persisting," "striving for accuracy," and "questioning and problem posing" (pp. 5–6).

The third CASEL competency, "social awareness," overlaps with "gather data through all senses" and "responding with wonderment and awe" (Alexander & Vermette, 2019, p. 6). The authors further suggested that the fourth CASEL competency, "relationship skills," would overlap with the HoM of "listening with understanding and empathy," "thinking and communicating with clarity and precision," and "thinking interdependently" (p. 6).

Alexander and Vermette (2019) believed that the fifth CASEL competency, "responsible decision-making," would overlap with the HoM of "taking responsible risks," "thinking flexibly," "applying past knowledge to new situations, "creating imagining, and innovating, and "finding humor" (pp. 6–7). The authors identified the HoM of "managing impulsivity" and "listening with understanding and empathy" as being the most important, particularly for middle school students. They recommended that teachers at the middle school level focus on them first, "as they open the doors to learning the other 14" (p. 7).

Altan et al. (2019) used qualitative content analysis to explore the relationship between the HoM and literature on educational theories related to intelligent behaviors. The educational theories that were linked to the various HoM included intelligent behaviors associated with Constructivism, Incremental Theory, Self-Regulated Learning Theory, Mindfulness, and Emotional Intelligence.

All of the HoM were associated with more than one theory (Altan et al., 2019). "The conclusion is that dispositions can be clustered around Habits of Mind that are related directly to educational learning theories vis-à-vis thoughtfulness, and to learning theories that support learning or mindfulness" (p. 169). The authors suggested that faculty in teacher education programs use the model to assist pre-service teachers in developing the HoM.

SUMMARY

The HoM developed by Costa and Kallick (2000) is gaining an impressive research base. Many researchers, from 2004 until 2021, have conducted studies on how the Habits of Mind have benefited elementary students, secondary students, and postsecondary students. In addition, researchers have conducted studies with teachers, superintendents, and prison inmates. Still other researchers have positioned the HoM in other bodies of literature. As researchers continue to investigate additional aspects related to the Habits of Mind, educators will know even more about the HoM and their impact on the educational community.

REFERENCES

Alexander, K., & Vermette, P. (2019). Implementing social and emotional learning standards by intertwining the Habits of Mind with the CASEL competencies. *Excelsior: Leadership in Teaching and Learning, 12*(1), 3–16.

Alhamlan, S., Aljasser, H., Almajed, A., Almansour, H., & Alahmad, N. (2018). A systematic review: Using Habits of Mind to improve student's [*sic*] thinking in class. *Higher Education Studies, 8*(1), 25–35. https://doi.org 10.5539/ hes. v8n1 p25

Altan, S., & Lane, J. F. (2018). Teachers' narratives: A source for exploring the influences of teachers' significant life experiences on their dispositions and teaching practices. *Teaching and Teacher Education, 74*(2018), 238–248. https://doi.org/10 .1016/j.tate.2018.05.012

Altan, S., Lane, J. F., & Dottin, E. (2019). Using Habits of Mind, intelligent behavior, and educational theories to create a conceptual framework for developing effective teaching dispositions. *Journal of Teacher Education, 70*(2), 169–183. DOI: 10.1177/0022487117736024

Bee, M. S. H., Seng, G. H., & Jusoff, K. (2013). Habits of Mind in the ESL classroom. *English Language Teaching, 6*(11), 130–138. http://dx.doi.org/10.5539/elt .v6n11p130

Burgess, J. (2012). The impact of teaching thinking skills as Habits of Mind to young children with challenging behaviors. *Emotional and Behavioural Difficulties, 17*(1), 47–63. http://dx.doi.org/10.1080/13632752.2012.652426

Chang, J. Y., Bautista, R., Filibeck, K. M., Wong, S. S., Nishimura, S., & Hishinuma, E. S. (2011). *Kailua High School Habits of Mind Inventory, 2005–2010.* University of Hawai'I at Manoa. Department of Psychiatry, Asian/Pacific Islander Youth Violence Prevention Center (APIYVPC).

CASEL (Collaborative for Academic, Social, and Emotional Learning). (2018). *Core SEL Competencies.* https://CASEL.org/core-competencies/

Costa, A., & Kallick, B. (2000). *Discovering and exploring Habits of Mind.* Association for Supervision and Curriculum Development.

Harper, J. (2020). *Habits of Mind of district administrators: An exploratory study* (Publication No. 27735131) [Doctoral dissertation, University of Wisconsin—Madison]. ProQuest Dissertations and Theses Global.

Hill, C. C. (2021). *Exploring Adult Basic Education student satisfaction: Influencing factors and programmatic responses* (Publication No. 28549177) [Doctoral dissertation, University of South Carolina]. ProQuest Dissertations and Theses Global.

Houston, M. C. (2009). Creating a workforce development culture to reduce reincarceration. *Transition and Offender Workforce Development Bulletin* (September). U.S. Department of Justice, National Institute of Corrections. http://nicic.gov/library/023065

Margeson, A. (2018). *Grade 9 teachers' perceptions of Habits of Mind and academic success* (Publication No. 13422299) [Doctoral dissertation, Walden University]. ProQuest Dissertations and Theses Global.

Marshall, A. R. (2004). *High school mathematics Habits of Mind instruction: Student growth and development* (Publication No. 1421654) [Masters thesis, Southwest Minnesota State University]. ProQuest Dissertations and Theses Global.

Matsuoka, C. J. (2007). *Thinking processes in middle-school students: Looking at Habits of the Mind and philosophy for Children Hawai'i* (Publication No. 3302153) [Doctoral dissertation, University of Hawai'i]. ProQuest Dissertations and Theses Global.

Muscott, P. G. (2018). *A study of the relationship between 'Habits of Mind' and 'Performance Task' achievement in an international school in South-east Asia* [Unpublished masters thesis]. University of Roehampton London.

O'Neill, P., Adler-Kassner, L., Fleischer, C., & Hall, A.-M. (2012). Symposium: On the framework for success in postsecondary writing. *College English, 74*(6), 520–533.

Owens, R. (2012). *New schools of thought: Developing thinking and learning communities.* [Unpublished doctoral dissertation]. Monash University, Clayton, VIC, Australia.

Royce, W. N. (2015). *An evaluation of the Habits of Mind character education program* (Publication No. 10161899) [Doctoral dissertation, Nova Southeastern University]. ProQuest Dissertations and Theses Global.

Shaeffer, J., Wong, F., O'Block, R., Locker, G., Eason, K., & Head, G. (2014). *Exploring Habits of Mind in the secondary science classroom.* University of Colorado Boulder.

Tabor, B., Brace, S., Lawrence, M., & Latti, A. (2008). The mindful culture of Waikiki Elementary School. In A. Costa & B. Kallick (Eds.), *Learning and leading with habits of mind: 16 Essential characteristics for success* (pp. 348–361). ASCD.

Teeple, S. K. (2021). *Exploring the relationship between social-emotional competencies and student outcomes in fully online learning environments* [Unpublished doctoral dissertation]. Gwynedd Mercy University.

Vazquez, J. C. (2020). *The impact of Habits of Mind: An exploratory study* (Publication No. 28156136) [Doctoral dissertation, Western Connecticut State University]. ProQuest Dissertations and Theses Global.

Workforce Development Partnership. (2013). Workforce Development Partnership. Waterbury, VT: Community High School of Vermont. http://doc.vermont.gov/programs/educational-programs/workforce-development-partnership

PART II

Creating Thoughtful and Mindful School Culture and Curriculum with Habits of Mind

Chapter 4

Building Cultures for Thinking

William A. Sommers

"Intentional cultures thrive when the simple systems put in place reinforce every cultural intention." —Richard Sheridan (2018), Chief Joy Officer

At Menlo Innovations in Ann Arbor, Michigan, Richard Sheridan is extremely intentional about building a culture that encourages and enhances a culture of learning. This includes all aspects of the organization from the hiring practices, policies, and procedures, and by extension, to the customers.

We know that schools are about learning. Can we replicate an intentional culture such as that at Menlo Innovations in our schools? This chapter is about how to create and sustain a culture of learning and thinking for all, including kids, colleagues, and community. Accelerating adult learning positively impacts student learning.

The culture of departments, grade levels, schools, or systems must exude an atmosphere of learning. The culture must also help kids, colleagues, and communities to create ways to learn or we will have isolated pockets of improvement. Teacher leaders, site administrators, and district officials are the leaders of learning and culture, but even other adults can model learning for the students' benefit. In fact, students are watching adults all the time to learn what is acceptable, what the boundaries of behaviors are, and how adults become successful.

It is important to know why accelerated learning is important, how it can be implemented constructively, and what the outcome will be. The "why" then, is accelerating learning for all. Based on the model of Simon Sinek's (2009) work, Start with Why, the "why" is a need for continual learning. The "how" is using the Art Costa and Bena Kallick' Habits of Mind (HoM) as a dashboard of possibilities to accelerate that learning and confront uncertainties.

The "what" is creating cultures that establish, enhance, and encourage accelerated learning for kids, colleagues, and community to deal with an ever-changing world.

NAVIGATING VUCA WITH HABITS OF MIND

VUCA stands for Volatility, Uncertainty, Complexity, and Ambiguity. As many people sit at home with limited options from a continuing COVID-19 crisis, the question is how do we respond in a VUCA world that does not seem to be changing any time soon? We want Vision, Understanding, Clarity, and Agility to successfully navigate these difficult times.

Within this respect, applying the Habits of Mind to VUCA is a great "How." More and more, business, government, and non-profits want and need levels of thinking that require creativity, collaboration, and communication. The table below provides a framework for four of the habits in each of the four parts of VUCA. Education, and the world for that matter, have been dealing with an increasing left side of this table (see Table 4.1). The right side of the table can be viewed as a pathway to mediate and manage the left side. The Habits of Mind provide specific behaviors to help people respond.

Table 4.1. VUCA Revisited

VUCA	Habits of Mind	VUCA Revisited
Volatility	Persisting	Vision
	Managing Impulsivity	
	Metacognition	
	Taking Responsible Risks	
Uncertainty	Listening with Understanding and Empathy	Understanding
	Thinking and Communicating with Clarity and Precision	
	Remaining Open to Continuous Learning	
	Thinking Interdependently	
Complexity (Confusion)	Applying Past Knowledge to New Situations	Clarity
	Finding Humor	
	Questioning and Problem Posing	
	Striving for Accuracy	
Ambiguity	Thinking Flexibly	Agility
	Gathering Data through All Your Senses	
	Creating, Imagining, and Innovating	
	Responding with Wonderment and Awe	

Volatility to Vision

COVID-19 is the latest event causing us to change the way we do things. Think about the effects of hurricanes, wars, viruses, global financial issues, and so on. Even when going to the moon, the spacecraft is off course much of the time but going to the moon is easier because we can see where we are going. That is why vision is so important. We may determine multiple ways to get where we want to go, but to reduce fear, anger, and volatility we need a vision for what we want. Habits that might help at this stage are:

- Persisting—When the vision is meaningful, it keeps us focused on the desired future. Knowing the destination helps keep us on track to our goal.
- Managing Impulsivity—Most people want to take action immediately. Think about the time, energy, money, and emotional costs of getting into a situation without thinking about the long-term consequences.
- Metacognition—Thinking about our thinking can help in that we generally react based on previous successful ideas. Once we learn other ways to think about issues, we can create multiple ways of framing an issue. Working with a diversity of ideas and people can help increase metacognition leading to better decisions. The more diversity, the better the idea generation.
- Taking Responsible Risks—Trying new things, wanting to accomplish new goals, and finding more effective ways to reach our vision involves leaving what may be comfortable and taking a risk. Smart people learn from what doesn't work as well as what does.

Uncertainty to Understanding

Most of us like certainty. People can find change to be disconcerting. But problems will continue to arise in our life. The only control is how we respond to them. Habits that might help at this stage are:

- Listening with Understanding and Empathy—When we listen to others, they tell us what they think and sometimes what beliefs drive their thoughts. Empathy generates a positive relationship which can provide even more learning from others. We share more with people we trust.
- Thinking and Communicating with Clarity and Precision—Asking questions that clarify thinking usually causes more clarity for me and the other person. The more precise the language, the better the communication.
- Thinking Interdependently—All work is in systems. At some point, we work and live with others. Others give us ideas, energy, and perspective.

Additionally, if we think both short-term and long-term, we can envision future consequences. School staff is interdependent with students, colleagues, and parents. We don't operate or live in a vacuum.

- Remaining Open to Continuous Learning—We need repertoire. The more strategies or skills we have, share with colleagues, and help students at different levels, the better we are prepared for the challenges ahead. I don't know of anyone who thinks that in the future we will be less diverse or have fewer problems to manage or that we can sit still while the world changes.

Complexity to Clarity

Life and problems are complex. One way to deal with complexity is to separate the problem into parts. Sometimes that works against us because so many problems are interconnected. Changing one part can create unintended consequences in another part. Therefore clarification of the issue is so critical. Making sure we keep the goals or vision in mind helps us make positive progress. Quick feedback loops are important to know what leading indicators can foreshadow results. Leading indicators, or formative assessments, give us a chance to change before results are in place. Habits that might help at this stage are:

- Applying Past Knowledge to New Situations—Past behavior can be helpful. Seeing new applications for existing problems can provide some solutions.
- Finding Humor—Humor has been shown to help creativity. There are techniques like Synectic and Improv that can help unleash creative thinking. Humor sometimes connects disconnected information and results in new clarity.
- Questioning and Problem Posing—Clarifying the problem is the first step. Questions will help this process. Questions also can surface assumptions, both positive and negative, to help clarify the goal. Unquestioned assumptions often lead to unintended consequences.
- Striving for Accuracy—This is where data can be extremely helpful but with a caveat: focus on the data that is relevant. Too often when gathering data, we drink from a fire hose. Instead, ask what data will help us know we are getting closer to a solution or farther away.

Ambiguity to Agility

In working with Scenario Planning, processes start with what is known, what we know we don't know, and what we don't know that we don't know. Be agile enough to look around at trends. To paraphrase former U.S. Secretary of Veterans Affairs, General Eric Shinseki, "If you don't like change, you are going to like irrelevance a lot less." This applies to so many current systems. Habits that might help at this stage are:

- Thinking Flexibly—Cultural anthropologist Mary Catherine Bateson wrote, "Life is improvisation." In other words, things happen that we don't anticipate or plan for. Therefore repertoire, and the ability to use that repertoire, is so important in education and life. Creativity and flexibility will help survive and thrive in all kinds of places.
- Gathering Data through All Your Senses—Checking our five senses can lead to additional ideas. We all have heard about visual, auditory, and kinesthetic learners. Don't forget the olfactory and gustatory senses. You might smell a rat or taste a bitter pill.
- Creating, Imagining, and Innovating—As we think about the future, this Habit of Mind will become even more important. How has technology progressed so quickly and made such an impact? How has the medical field saved more lives and prevented many diseases?
- Responding with Wonderment and Awe—Stopping to reflect and focus on how far we have come is important. Stop to smell the roses.

SUMMARY

Start with WHY. The short answer is freedom. More learning in both knowledge and skills gives a person more options in employment, in personal satisfaction, and keeping creative for an unknown future. VUCA will continue to challenge individuals and organizations now and in the future. If you know the "why," we can find the "how."

HOW. The Habits of Mind provide learning processes that are long-term transferrable skills. HoM is valuable for college (extended learning of all kinds), careers (that will continue to evolve), and communities (where continual challenges exist). Knowing the why and how, what do we want?

WHAT. Better people, better communities, and ultimately, a better world. When individuals or organizations deplete ideas and processes to solve problems, conflict results. What we want are self-directed learners that can adapt to changing environments and positively contribute to a better planet. So, the challenge is not only knowing this but putting these strategies into practice. To quote Angeles Arrien: "If your goals is to wake up the dead, GET UP, TODAY IS A WORKDAY." Namaste.

REFERENCES

Bateson, M. (1989). *Composing a life*. New York: Atlantic Monthly Press.

Costa, A., & Kallick, B. (2000). *Habits of Mind.* Alexandria, VA: ASCD.

Dintersmith, Ted. (2018). *What school could be.* Princeton, NJ: Princeton University Press.

Frank, C., & Magnone, P. (2011). *Drinking from the fire hose: Making smarter decisions without drowning in information.* London: Penguin.

Goldsmith, M. (2007). *What got you here won't get you there.* New York: Hyperion.

Johansen, Bob. (2007). *Get there early.* San Francisco: Berrett-Kohler.

Marshak, R. (2006). *Covert processes at work.* San Francisco: Berrett-Kohler.

Sheridan, Richard. (2018). *Chief joy officer.* New York: Portfolio/Penguin.

Sinek, Simon. (2009). *Start with why.* New York: Penguin.

Wagner, Tony, & Dintersmith, Ted. (2015). *Most likely to succeed.* New York: Scribner.

Chapter 5

Building the School Culture with Habits of Mind

Arthur L. Costa, Bena Kallick, and Allison Zmuda

"The learning organization is a place where people continually expand their capacity to create the results they truly desire, where new and expansive patterns of thinking are nurtured, where collective aspiration is set free, and where people are continually learning how to learn together."

—Peter Senge

The Habits of Mind are foundational to building a school culture that operates as a learning organization. In such a culture, we see how the Habits of Mind flourish in the hearts, minds, and actions of all its people. There is a sense of belonging. A place where each member is valued and their voice is encouraged and invited to the table to take the lead in problem solving and innovative thinking. Differences are seen as strengths, and there is a dedication to the well-being of all members of the school community.

Over the past 30 years, we have witnessed the profound transformation of numerous schools' cultures into powerful learning organizations when they make a commitment to Habits of Mind as a crucial part of their vision. We believe a school's culture will benefit when students—and teachers—develop the Habits of Mind, which are as cognitively demanding as any technical "skill." Over time, as everyone in the school becomes effective in employing the dispositions described in this book, positive interactions and practices will pervade the school.

When everyone in a school agrees that it's as essential for students to develop these dispositions as it is to gain academic abilities, that's a powerful shared vision for students' future lives. The habits develop the capacities of

45

the entire school community to recognize and apply this dispositional thinking to the curriculum, when meeting unpredictable challenges, and to guide the many decisions that a school staff must make. Members of the school community learn to confront problematic situations by asking themselves, "What is the most *intelligent thing I can do right now?*"

SEVEN KEY FACTORS TO GROW THE CULTURE

There are seven key factors that contribute to a school culture grounded in the Habits of Mind. They are: (1) Common, Consistent Vocabulary; (2) Social Norming and Responsibility; (3) Public Practice; (4) Mutual Indicators of Growth; (5) Community and Parents as Partners; (6) A Shared Vision of Graduates; and (7) Committed Leadership. These seven key factors work in concert with one another, to create *attention density*: a neuroscientific condition in which the density of experience—focusing often enough, long enough, and intense enough—can change neural pathways and brain circuitry (Rock & Swartz, 2006). Each will be explored below.

Common, Consistent Vocabulary

The Habits of Mind provide a common language that anchors communication throughout the school community. Whether conversing with students, parents, administrators, members of the community or each other, the vocabulary provides consistency when describing and` recognizing the challenges, aspirations, celebrations, and concepts that pervade daily work in the school. As children hear the language and link the terms with the observed behaviors of the adults, they soon realize that "this is how we do things around here"; so they, too, begin to use the language of the Habits of Mind with their peers in the classroom, on the playground and at home.

Social Norming and Responsibility

Social norms are informal understandings that govern the behavior of members of an organization. Social norms can be thought of as rules that prescribe what people should and should not do given their social surroundings (Donohoo et al., 2018) as they learn to live the Habits of Mind. An example follows.

The principal invites one of the teachers to facilitate the next faculty meeting (Garmston & McKanders, 2021). She opens the meeting with an agenda listing the problems and decisions that the staff must resolve. After welcoming the staff and sharing other pleasantries, she begins by asking, "If these are the problems we face today, which Habits of Mind will serve us as we work together to respond to them?" The staff generates a list, and, after the meeting ends, the staff reflects on which Habits of Mind served them as they approached each problem and which Habits of Mind could be improved upon.

- "We will need to listen with understanding and empathy to each other's points of view."
- "We will need to think flexibly and generate many ways of solving these problems."
- "We will need to persist. Some of these problems have been plaguing us for some time."
- "Let's remember to find a little humor and laugh together!"

Mutual Indicators of Growth

Because staff members co-create a common commitment to producing student growth in the Habits of Mind, they dialogue about indicators they observe students initiating and performing as they progress through the grades (Kallick & Zmuda, 2017). They report to each other such indicators as:

- During the student council meeting, Danielle, the student body president, advocated for the use of listening with understanding and empathy to each other's point of view as she conducted the meeting.
- At one Habits of Mind school, eighth graders adopt learning buddies from kindergarten and first grade. The eighth and first graders read stories together and found examples of the Habits of Mind. Today, they were reading *Charlotte's Web* and discussed how the pig needed to manage its impulsivity. (Costa & Kallick, 2018)
- Matt, as a third grader, complained there was too much emphasis on the Habits of Mind. No matter where he turned, he said, they reappeared. Now, Matt, as a sixth grader, realized the importance of listening with understanding and empathy after he visited homeless people and heard stories of their plight.

In addition, the whole school community pays attention to how they use the habits in their meetings. Surveys, focus groups and other strategies help the organization stay focused on soliciting feedback and remaining open to continuous learning.

When staff members, parents, and students collectively embrace the Habits of Mind and work together to model, recognize, and reinforce these habits, they begin to realize their positive effects. This feeling of confidence in themselves—belief in their mission, and value of their actions—produces a "collective efficacy" which John Hattie (2016) placed at the top of his list of factors that influence student achievement.

A Shared Vision of Graduates

When teachers were asked to write a letter of recommendation for a graduating student who is applying for college entrance, military service or a career placement, the Habits of Mind provide a rich way of describing the attributes that employers welcome, such as: precise, thoughtful, humorous, empathic, creative, eager learners; persistent, collaborative, creative, problem solvers; and flexible thinkers. School staff and parents could easily agree that these are the dispositions desired not only for graduates, but also for the school's teachers and administrators themselves.

Public Practice

Some school staffs work in silos. They seldom interact with teachers from other departments about strategies they use in teaching their subject area. World language teachers, for example, seldom discuss their issues with mathematics teachers, and the music staff rarely interacts with computer science techies. In Habits of Mind schools, however, all staff members make their practice public to one another because they share a common vision of their graduates. Each subject area group finds ways of building the Habits of Mind into their curriculum (Costa & Kallick, 2009) by providing settings in which students can transfer and apply relevant Habits of Mind.

Creating, innovating, and imagining, for example, is applied not only in their artwork but also in the robotics lab and in poetry classes as well. The dispositions are what are taught, valued, and assessed on the journey towards mastery of their content (Louis et al., 1996).

Parents and Community as Partners

It is much more likely that students will learn and practice the Habits of Mind if they witness their parents and community members dialoguing about and exhibiting Habits of Mind as well. They describe how they need to listen, to pose questions, to think creatively and to persist in their work.

- In one secondary school, the students invited business leaders from the community to share the Habits of Mind with them and to value the necessity for their employees using the Habits of Mind in performing their work.

- One parent shared this insight: "We do talk about the Habits of Mind as a family, and I share them with friends because I find them to be pertinent and applicable in many situations. I admire how the Habits of Mind reinforce and emphasize all of the characteristics that we value so highly."
- Another parent commented, "After I made some cookies, I told Peter he had to wait until after dinner to have one, to which he replied, 'I am *managing my impulsivity* for sure!'"
- When Habits of Mind were explored in the business community, Emergency Medical Services (EMS) providers in Kettle Moraine, WI, identified that finding humor was essential due to the enormous amount of stress the job requires.

Committed Leadership

The greatest power that leaders have is that they can influence the narrative of the school. If the narrative focuses on current educational fads, test scores, and compliance with mandates, then that is what is perceived as the importance of learning. In such schools, students learn to get to class on time, raise their hand when they wish to speak or ask a question, and listen to the teacher. Instead, if the narrative is becoming aware of and controlling thinking processes, what it means to be an empathic listener, and what alternative strategies might be generated to solve problems, then teachers and students learn to perceive learning in a different way.

This reframes how teachers and students view learning: one that requires responding intelligently to challenges, having strategies to comprehend and tackle complex problems, and viewing setbacks as opportunities for learning (Donohoo et al., 2018).

CREATING A HABITS OF MIND CULTURE

The interplay of the seven key factors creates a culture in which there is a density of repetitions and recognitions. The Habits of Mind define the behaviors of the culture. As students progress through the elementary grades, or as they engage in learning the various subject matters at the high school, there is a recurring focus on the Habits of Mind. No matter where they turn, whether it be in social studies class, science lab or football field, the kindergarten or any other grade-level classroom, their teachers invite them to focus on one or more of the Habits of Mind as they engage with the content.

Signals and posters throughout the school and classroom remind the staff, students, and parents about the value of the Habits of Mind. Newsletters to the community and reports to parents not only define the Habits of Mind but also share indicators of student progress and educate the wider community. Waikiki School in Honolulu calls itself the Mindful School. The music teacher composed a special song that the students sing at assemblies and each year they adopt student-designed Habits of Mind t-shirts (Tabor et al., 2008).

Some schools recognize students with awards, badges or bracelets for their performance of one or more of the habits (Costa & Kallick, 2019, p. 51). The more students focus on and grapple with the Habits of Mind, the more they learn to believe in themselves. The habits become internalized into their hearts, minds, and behaviors. The success of a Habits of Mind School culture lies in the critical nature of collaboration and the strength of believing in and fostering Habits of Mind so that together—administrators, faculty, parents, and students—can achieve magnificent and sustainable outcomes (Tabor, 2019).

REFERENCES

Costa A., & Kallick, B. (2009). *Habits of mind across the curriculum*. Alexandria, VA: ASCD.

Costa, A., & Kallick, B. (2008). *Leading and learning with Habits of Mind: 16 characteristics for success.* Alexandria, VA: ASCD.

Costa, A., & Kallick, B. (2019). *Nurturing habits of mind in early childhood.* Alexandria, VA: ASCD.

Donohoo, J., Hattie, J., & Eells, R. (March 2018). The power of collective efficacy. *Educational Leadership, 75*(6), 40–44.

Garmston, R., & McKanders, C. (2021). *It's your turn: Teachers as facilitators.* Burlington, VT: MiraVia.

Hattie, J. (July 2016). *Mindframes and maximizers.* 3rd Annual Visible Learning Conference held in Washington, DC.

Kallick, B., & Zmuda, A. (2017). *Students at the center: Personalizing learning and Habits of Mind.* Alexandria, VA: ASCD.

Leithwood, K. (1992). The move towards transformational leadership. *Educational Leadership,* Feb., 8–12.

Louis, K., Marks, H., & Kruse, S. (1996). Teacher's professional community in restructuring schools. *American Educational Research Journal, 33*(4), 757–798.

Tabor, B. (2019). Creating a mindful schoolwide culture to maximize learning. In A. Costa and B. Kallick (Eds.), *Nurturing habits of mind in early childhood classrooms.* Alexandria, VA: ASCD.

Tabor, B., Brace, S., Lawrence, M., & Latti, A. (2008). The mindful culture of Waikiki Elementary School. In A. Costa and B. Kallick (Eds.), *Leading and learning with Habits of Mind: 16 characteristics for success.* Alexandria, VA: ASCD.

Chapter 6

Impacting Change through the Habits of Mind

Priscila Freitas Torres

The future of learning is not about teaching content in isolation; however, it is about knowing how to apply the dispositions of understanding to make new connections, develop new perspectives, and solve personal, local, and global problems. To impact change in any school the Habits of Mind (HoM) need to be part of its DNA. Habits of Mind are the vehicle through which learning competencies, skills, and understandings are cultivated (OECD, 2030). HoM should be woven into the everyday actions to be living and breathing inside the learning environment.

Once the decision is made that the HoM will serve as a foundational pillar of the school and its programs, a common language needs to be established. These habits become part of this known dialect that is familiar and natural to all members of the community, to include learners, educators, leadership, staff, families, and anyone who comes into contact with the school. This chapter is dedicated to any school who seeks to impact action through HoM. In the following pages, the case study of the Escola Concept group of schools is used to inspire and illustrate this journey to make it tangible and applicable for any community.

There are five aspects that will contribute to the HoM being front and center in all learning communities: a focused and supportive mission statement; a clear vision; structured professional learning moments for faculty, staff, and families; scheduled opportunities for thoughtful collaboration and dedicated planning time; and the documentation of the learning process. These specific actions will lead to the successful establishment of a culture where the Habits of Mind are valued, visible, and actively promoted.

In this chapter, these five aspects are discussed in detail to offer any member of a school community or leader insightful strategies to lead this movement to positively impact action in a learning ecosystem.

FOCUSED AND SUPPORTIVE MISSION STATEMENT

The institution's mission statement should concisely articulate its purpose. When considering mission statements, terms such as action-oriented goals, core values, competencies, cohesiveness, foundation, and compass come to mind. If the HoM will be used to impact change in the school, it must be mentioned in the mission statement. The mission statement will set the foundation and the groundwork for developing a common language within the school, while guiding its stakeholders to coalesce around understanding the Habits, its impact, and its importance to the community.

Guiding questions such as:

- What does the school offer?
- Why does the school offer what it offers?
- What is the school's program designed to do?
- How does the school educate the twenty-first century learner?
- What is the ultimate goal of the education offered by the school?

. . . may support writing a mission statement that will impact change and bring the Habits of Mind to center stage to impact positive change and transformation within the ecosystem of the school. Schools can use the following guiding questions and responses to support a missions statement that will impact change the Habits of Mind.

- *What does the school offer?* An academically rigorous, challenging, inclusive, global education.
- *Why does the school offer what it offers?* To develop happy and thoughtful human beings who positively impact the world we live in.
- *What is the school's program designed to do?* The school's program is designed to nurture the dispositions of lifelong learners who collaborate to co-create, embrace an entrepreneurial mindset, understand the meaning of living sustainably, and are globally and digitally fluent.
- *How does the school educate the twenty-first century learner?* Learners apply habits of mind to their daily actions, use the language of thinking to communicate, and understand the elements of design thinking to problem solve and innovate. Learning is facilitated and assessed through relevant, project-based experiences.

- *What is the ultimate goal of the education offered by the school?* Upon graduation, learners will be prepared for their university of choice in Brazil, or elsewhere around the world.

In the example above, the Habits of Mind are mentioned to describe how the school will educate the twenty-first century learner. Using this statement as a springboard to action, the school will deconstruct the meaning of "Questioning and Problem Posing," one of the Habits of Mind, and reflect upon this statement. This exercise can be done using all of the statements in the mission, as it will link what the school is proposing to deliver, which can be defined as its value proposition, to the school's actions.

Questions that can support unpacking this discussion may include:

- What are the proof points for each of the statements in the mission?
- How will learners apply the Habits of Mind to their daily actions?
- What will the application of the Habits of Mind as daily actions look like for learners in different age levels?

Once the mission statement is written, and unpacked with all the stakeholders, it will need to become enculturated into the daily life of the school. Enculturation begins with rituals that will allow for the practices to be purposefully repeated to become part of the fabric of the school. The mission will contribute to instill trust, respect, and knowledge of what the school currently does, how it addresses pain points, promotes culture, and makes big picture strategies public.

Clear Vision

A clear mission statement will support the vision. If the mission is defined as the journey, then the vision can be defined as the destination. Using the example highlighted on Table 6.1, which states, "learners apply Habits of Mind to their daily actions," in the vision statement the result of learners applying these Habits to their daily actions could be, " . . . to nurture confidence in each child to be a doer, a cutting-edge thinker and to have a growth mindset to take responsible risks, while accepting failure as part of the learning process." The vision statement is aspirational; however it is crucial for the mission statement to address the HOW.

As the school evolves and its goals are met, its vision might change to incorporate future goals that will lead to new innovations. The guiding question is usually, "How does a school ensure it's fulfilling its mission so that it can reach its vision, or at least become closer to reaching its vision?" Clearly

Table 6.1. Assessment Considerations

Considerations	Assessment for Learning	Assessment as Learning	Assessment of Learning
Why Assess?	To enable educators to determine next steps in advancing learning	To guide and provide opportunities for each student to monitor and critically reflect on learning and identify next steps	To certify or inform parents or others of students' proficiency in relation to curriculum learning outcomes
Assess What?	Each student's progress and learning in relation to curricular outcomes	Each student's thinking about learning, what strategies are used to support/challenge learning and the mechanisms used to adjust and advance learning	The extent to which a student can apply the key concepts, knowledge, skills, and attitudes related to curricular outcomes
What Methods?	A range of methods in different modes that make students' skills and understanding visible	A range of methods in different modes that elicit students' learning and metacognitive processes	A range of methods in different modes that assess both product and process
Ensuring Quality	Accuracy and consistency of observations and interpretations of student learning Clear, detailed learning expectations Accurate, detailed notes for descriptive feedback to each student	Accuracy and consistency of student's self-reflections, self-monitoring, and self-adjustment Engagement of the student in considering and challenging thinking Students record their own learning	Accuracy, consistency, and fairness of judgements based on high-quality information Clear, detailed learning expectations Fair and accurate summative reporting

Using the Information	Provide students with accurate, descriptive feedback to further learning	Provide each student with accurate, descriptive feedback that will help him/her develop independent learning habits	Indicate each student's level of learning
	Differentiate instruction by continually checking where the student is in relation to curricular outcomes	Have each student focus on learning (not in getting the right answer)	Provide the foundation for discussions on placement or promotion
	Provide parents/guardians with descriptive feedback about student learning and ideas for support	Provide each student with ideas for adjusting, rethinking, and articulating learning	Report fair, accurate, and detailed information that can be used to decide next steps in a student's learning
		Provide the conditions for the teacher and student to discuss alternatives	
		Students report about their learning	

defined objectives and parameters support individuals and schools alike to achieve set goals eliminating ambiguity, while setting a clear timeframe, checking for progress, and celebrating milestones. The vision can be seen as the school's goal, where the school wants to get to. If it's the destination, then a clear path needs to be set to get there.

This evolutionary path can be framed within the school's Academic Strategic Plan, which is a documented roadmap of how the school plans to achieve its goals to include the targets to achieve them. Planning backwards and beginning with the end in mind are strategies that may support this journey. A self-assessment rubric designed by the school with specific "look fors" can incorporate the elements that need to be met by the school so the school can reach its targets.

STRUCTURED PROFESSIONAL LEARNING MOMENTS FOR FACULTY, STAFF, AND FAMILIES

A community of lifelong learners is represented by all its members having continuous opportunities to grow their learning, thinking, and understanding. The educational experience of each child in the community is impacted by all its members, therefore all the members of the community, independent of their role or position, need to understand the foundational educational pillars valued by the school. This can be done through professional development/ learning meetings and webinars, schoolwide initiatives such as the Habit of Mind of the month, the Institute for the Habits of Mind accreditation, and action research opportunities.

Professional Development/Learning for the Internal Community

When planning the yearlong professional development or professional learning (PD/PL) calendar, the first step is to include Habits of Mind in the PD/PL cycle. Research from Learning Forward and Mizell supports that dedicated learning time of two to three times a week should be offered for schools and teams to support their learning goals. In the case study of the Escola Concept group of schools, at least one meeting a month was dedicated to developing a common understanding about the Habits.

A designated leader was appointed to prepare the PD/PL content, organize the experience for the educators, and create accountability systems to ensure that educators were weaving the language of Habits to daily experiences and teachings. All the educators in the school were also signed up to participate in the Eduplanet 21 Habits of Mind course to learn the theory that supports the Habits and to make connections of how to bridge theory and practice.

During direct instruction about the Habits, educators intentionally articulate the Habit of Mind in focus and connect it to its definition, in addition to highlighting the behaviors that are linked to making the Habit visible during our daily lives. All these actions contribute to the Habits of Mind being used to build and develop community. The ritual of speaking in the language of Habits may be used to define the culture of the school. Some examples of initiatives that involve building community with the Habits of Mind center stage are shared below.

Habit of Mind of the Month

A calendar may be developed to determine which of the Habits of Mind will be the focus of each month. The ultimate goal is to raise awareness about the Habits of Mind among the community. Other benefits of this action include:

- Develop synergy around the study of the Habits. The community will be focused on the same habit and generate momentum about actions to promote it.
- Systematic approach to ensure that all classes and all learners study each Habit during a specific timeframe.

- Campus wide study about the Habits to increase collaboration in growing the resources for multiple age groups.
- Habits being made visible on the walls, in the hallways, and in conversations. Learners and educators make connections to the Habits as they develop a Habits of Mind culture and establish a common language.
- Common focus for the school's digital magazine/newsletter, expanding the synergy and the discussion to the broader school community.
- Learning/Inspiration Commons with book displays to address the theme for the specific Habit, deepening the understanding through literature and research.

Teachable Moments

In addition to direct instruction, educators may use specific teachable moments in class to bring awareness to a specific Habit of Mind in focus. Some examples include:

- A class is sharing highlights about the day during circle time and one child begins to interrupt the child who is speaking. The educator can use this moment to remind the group that listening with understanding and empathy is a class norm and that mental energy needs to be dedicated to show respect for who is speaking. This is a strong opportunity for the educator to model the disposition that before each person shares his thoughts he needs to share how it connects to what the previous person was sharing.
  - This allows the group to begin to develop the connection between the habits of mind and the language of thinking. When using the language of thinking, learners will use verbs such as connect, explore, extend, investigate, to further the thinking of conversations.
- A group of kids is out for break time and they are upset because they want to play in the treehouse and there's a huge line. They express their frustration to their educator and mention they only want to play in the tree house and they don't want to play with any other equipment in the playground. The educator takes this moment to share that they should take a responsible risk and venture out to the rocket toy to experiment with something different and have a new experience.
- Class is coming to an end and the educator asks the group to think about their thinking and report on their learning about two-step equations. Learners are asked to respond to the following prompts:
  - I really understood how to . . .
  - I need more information about . . .
  - A question I still have is . . .

Parent Education/Learning for Families

Learning is a social endeavor, as stated by Patricia Kuhl (2018). A child's education is a team effort that can be visually depicted using the image of a pyramid. Each side of the pyramid represents a specific stakeholder, family, child, and school.

If the child spends equal amounts of time in school and at home, it is important that the school leverages the power of the family in the education process. Using the Escola Concept case study, a series of Parent Education/ Learning sessions were regularly planned and scheduled to focus on educating families about the Habits of Mind.

These moments included, an introduction to Habits of Mind (learning and familiarizing families with each of the Habits), how to identify behaviors and develop language around the Habits, sharing anecdotes of how children are using the Habits at school, sharing videos of children demonstrating specific dispositions and identifying how these could be directly related to the Habits, and showcasing movies in which learners had to identify moments when characters used a specific Habit to reach a goal.

The monthly school newsletter also featured Habits of Mind with tips on how to grow the Habits of Mind at school and at home, alongside the Parent Educational Learning Community initiative where articles were shared with families once a month and a scheduled date was set for members to come to campus (or online) for a one hour protocol-based meeting to discuss the article. These actions contributed to growing the thinking, knowledge, and understanding of the greater community about the Habits.

Institute for the Habits of Mind Accreditation

The accreditation process is a structured opportunity for the school to show its commitment to the Habits of Mind. Deciding to go in this direction is a formal way to state that the Habits are aligned to the values of the school and to the foundation in which learning is built. One of the greatest benefits of the accreditation is the self-study in which the community uses the official rubrics developed by the Institute for the Habits of Mind to self-assess its current state and develop an action plan as to how to meet the external goals set by the Institute.

This reflective process will support the community to seek intentionality and purpose when addressing and defining its beliefs, behaviors, and actions. Following the self study, a roadmap is developed of how the specific goals will be achieved, how external professional training will be led, when dedicated schoolwide professional learning moments will happen, why focused events and actions will take place, and finally it will lead to the opportunity to re-assess growth.

Ultimately the accreditation process offers the school formal recognition of its accomplishments, spotlights areas of growth/change, provides substantial information for informed decision making, while also formally placing the school in a community alongside other international schools where the Habits of Mind are valued, cultivated, and developed toward a larger educational goal.

Action Research Opportunities

Robert Marzano (2008) compares the role of an educator to that of a medical practitioner. Marzano states that knowledge is built when sifting through cases and studies. Patients and doctors, like educators, need to understand which of the effective strategies that they read about make sense for the community they are impacting.

Action research can be the answer to develop this continuous and relevant knowledge base. When action research emerged in the 1950s, it filled the gap between academic research and its daily application. Action research is connected to agency, which comes from taking the time to ask what works and approaching this curiosity with testing to try to answer that question.

For the purpose of growing a research mindset through the Habits of Mind, in the Escola Concept case study, the action research focused on a specific habit. Individually or in small groups, educators and leaders explored questions that involved a Habit of Mind.

A few ideas for research included:

- How can educators encourage learners to have a questioning attitude?
- What does persistence look like in the early years learning space?
- How can teenagers be engaged in the dispositions of creating, imagining, and innovating?

Action Research is part of the Institute for the Habits of Mind accreditation rubric with the goal for schools to enculturate a lifelong learning and research mindset in its practices, as part of its day-to-day experiences, occurring regularly, informing learning, and contributing to the school planning and review.

SCHEDULED OPPORTUNITIES FOR THOUGHTFUL COLLABORATION AND DEDICATED PLANNING TIME

Schedules dictate the culture of the school. The schedule shares intended messages, such as that of the timetable, which includes where learners need to go when and what classes they will be attending. The schedule also shares unintended messages, such as the values and beliefs of the school.

Questions such as:

- How is the daily cadence of the school organized to maximize learning and collaboration?
- How are the names of the classes connected to the learning that is happening?
- Is there dedicated time for collaborative planning when grade level teams will come together to contribute, question, think, and make decisions?

Collaboration is the foundation for many successful businesses to flourish. In the start-up culture, there are limited projects without collaborative actions. When considering schools, psylos may become common when purposeful leadership is not in place to promote productive sharing of knowledge, skills, and understanding. Ideally schools should create schedules that reflect the culture they are willing to promote. To develop a culture where Habits of Mind are valued, visible, and actively promoted, time is of essence and so is communication.

Time needs to be set aside in the schedule for educators to communicate and collaborate with principals and/or teaching and learning coaches to have directed conversations about how to plan using the Habits of Mind, how to develop meaningful lessons that will focus on developing the Habits, how to weave the Habits into the culture of the school, and how the Habits will be connected to the content level knowledge that needs to be developed for all subject areas.

Clear expectations and guidelines for educators will support success during the scheduled opportunities for collaboration. Developing collaborative teams involves building autonomy and sharing what collaboration looks like, feels like, and sounds like, and what are the goals to be achieved through the collaborative actions. In this way, teams can come together, focus on the end goal, and meet with the leadership to lapidate outcomes.

DOCUMENTATION OF LEARNING

When learning takes place, documentation needs to happen. Documentation of learning is connected to making learning visible through assessment. There are three categories of assessments: assessment of learning, for learning, and as learning. These assessment categories should continuously be taken into consideration, even when the focus is on the Habit of Mind. The purpose is to bring tangibility to the learning of a social emotional component of the curriculum, which includes the Habits.

Table 6.1 addresses five general considerations from Principals' Training Center, 2009 about assessment which will contribute to strengthening the culture of Habits of Mind in any community.

Once the educator has clarity about the purpose of the assessment, then the process of documenting learning becomes more natural. The product should reflect the learners' understanding about the Habits of Mind.

It is important for educators to consider the Habits of Mind as a curricular component, comparable to any subject level knowledge. Clear learning outcomes, expectations, and success criteria need to be developed so that there is direction to where the learning of the Habits of Mind is headed. The relevance of intentionally learning about the Habits of Mind cannot be overlooked when addressing it as a social emotional component of the curriculum.

Learners need to be able to recognize, identify, and define the Habits of Mind, articulate why they are important to learning, make connections to their dispositions, and be able to incorporate the dispositions of the Habits into their daily lives. For this to happen, they need to intentionally learn about the Habits of Mind as part of the curriculum. Learning about the Habits of Mind can also be made visible through the connection with Visible Thinking Routines. An example of how this can be done includes:

Visible Thinking Routines: Color-Symbol-Image Combined with What Makes You Say That?

- What COLOR best represents persisting to you? Why did you choose this color?
- What SYMBOL best represents persisting to you? Why did you choose this symbol?
- What IMAGE best represents persisting to you? Why did you choose this image?

Both Thinking Routines can be combined for learners to engage in metacognitive processes making their thinking visible and also providing the

Table 6.2. Self-Assessment Habits of Mind Rubric

Habits	Exemplary Habits	Meets Expectations	Approaches Expectations	Developing Expectations
Persisting	I consistently stick to a task and am persistent. I am focused. I strive to reach my goal.	I stick to the task most of the time and am somewhat persistent. I focus quite often, and I seek ways to reach my goal.	I stick to the task some of the time; sometimes I have to be reminded to keep on task. I could improve my focus. Sometimes I give up.	I rarely stick to a task. I need to be more persistent and focus more. I get upset when the answer to a problem is not immediately known.
Managing Impulsivity	I think before I act. I form a vision of the product, plan of action, or goal. I consistently consider consequences and alternatives. I remain calm, thoughtful, and deliberate.	Most of the time I think before I act. Sometimes I consider consequences and alternatives. Most of the time I remain calm, thoughtful, and deliberate.	I frequently interrupt and blurt out in class. Sometimes I think before I act. I need to improve on controlling my impulses in a more mature manner.	I blurt out the first answer that comes to mind. I rarely consider alternatives. I make judgments before fully understanding the problem. I rarely control my impulses.

| Listening to Others with Understanding and Empathy | I spend a large amount of time listening. I can accurately paraphrase another person's idea. I can detect emotional states in oral and body language. I understand diverse perspectives. | Sometimes I listen to others. Sometimes I can paraphrase another person's idea. Sometimes I can read body language. I try to understand many different perspectives, but I could improve. | I seldom listen to others. If I'm interested, I can partially paraphrase another person's idea. I don't care about body language. I need to improve on understanding other people's points of view. | I ridicule, laugh at, and put down the ideas of others. I find it challenging to build upon another person's ideas. I rehearse what to say instead of truly listening. I rarely try to consier a different point of view. |

educator the opportunity of collectively displaying the thinking of the class to make the group's thinking visible to the entire community. The process of making thinking visible engages all members in a community wide metacognitive process about the Habits of Mind. As the halls are walked, the walls speak to those who are passing.

Self-assessment rubrics are another tool to document the evolution of the learning process. When considering these rubrics, the focus is on assessment as learning. Table 6.2. depicts an example of a rubric for Persisting, Managing Impulsivity, and Listening with Understanding and Empathy that can be used with middle school learners.

SUMMARY: IMPACTING CHANGE

Vigorous school communities are solid ecosystems of learning characterized by embedded rituals which define the culture beyond the learning of content. The Habits of Mind is the foundational pillar that will impact positive change in a school. It outlives content and focuses on developing dispositions of successful individuals. Habits of Mind are about developing capacity, motivation, creativity, and communication. They speak to the interconnectedness of parts. Value is no longer built by vertical relationships between teacher and student, but by horizontal networks built upon connections, collaboration, and communication. Learning is defined beyond content acquisition and the Habits of Mind are the connector between the values of the school and the dispositions needed for children to grow into successful adults. A supportive mission statement, a clear vision, structured professional learning moments for faculty, staff and families, scheduled opportunities for thoughtful collaboration and dedicated planning time, and the documentation of the learning process, are the five aspects to impact change which were discussed in this chapter. Combined, these comprise the foundation for transformation and the tracking of positive results.

REFERENCES

Bambi Betts. (2009). *PTC assessing student learning*. Miami, FL: Principals' Training Center.

Costa, A. L., & Kallick, B. (2009). *Habits of mind across the curriculum: Practical and creative strategies for teachers*. Association for Supervision and Curriculum Development.

Costa, A. L., & Kallick, B. (2018). *Learning and leading with habits of mind: 16 essential characteristics for success*. Association for Supervision and Curriculum Development.

Dweck, C. (2017). *Mindset: Changing the way you think to fulfill your potential*. Robinson.

Gladwell, M. (2019). *Outliers: The story of success*. Back Bay Books, Little, Brown and Company.

Johnson, C. A. (February 2022). *Leading change*. Mumbai.

Kuhl, P. (July 25, 2018). *Learning and the social brain*. Edutopia. Retrieved February 1, 2022, from https://www.edutopia.org/package/learning-and-social-brain

Learning Forward, & Mizell, Hayes. (2010). Why professional development matters. *Learning Forward*, Learning Forward, learningforward.org/wp-content/uploads/2017/08/professional-development-matters.pdf.

Marzano, R. J. (2007). Using action research and local models of instruction to enhance teaching. *Journal of Personnel Evaluation in Education, 20*(3–4), 117–128. https://doi.org/10.1007/s11092-008-9058-7

OECD. (2022). OECD. www.oecd.org/education/2030-project/teaching-and-learning/learning/attitudes-and-values/Attitudes_and_Values_for_2030_concept_note.pdf

Perkins, D. N. (2009). *Making learning whole: How seven principles of teaching can transform education*. Jossey-Bass.

Ritchhart, R., & Perkins, D. (2008, February). Making thinking visible. *Educational Leadership*. Retrieved January 13, 2022, from http://www.pz.harvard.edu/sites/default/files/Thinking%20Routine%20Matrix_3.pdf

Ritchhart, R., Church, M., & Morrison, K. (2011). *Making thinking visible: How to promote engagement, understanding, and independence for all learners*. Jossey-Bass.

Schleicher, A. (2010). *The case for 21st-century learning*. OECD. Retrieved November 20, 2021, from https://www.oecd.org/general/thecasefor21st-centurylearning.htm

Tishman, S., & Palmer, P. (2005). Visible thinking. *Leadership Compass*.

Chapter 7

Teacher Servant Leadership and Habits of Mind

A Connected Framework

Julio Vazquez and Jody S. Piro

After reading this chapter, you will have an understanding of the connections between teacher servant leadership and Habits of Mind and how these frameworks work together to promote teacher leadership which results in student success. Teacher-leaders are instrumental in creating the changes that are needed for students to succeed (Fiarman, 2017). For students to succeed beyond school, changes in our educational systems must occur that include keeping up with the pace of change of twenty-first century workforce demands; globalization; a service economy; citizenship; and technology (Kay & Greenhill, 2012).

Administrative leadership alone is insufficient to create needed change because leadership is not defined as solely positional in nature but for optimal effectiveness, leadership in schools needs to be distributed informally (Darling-Hammond et al., 1995). Teacher-leaders who are able to employ thinking dispositions so they can effectively impact their environment and serve and lead others are essential to learning institutions (Costa & Kallick, 2008).

Costa and Kallick (2008) found that school leaders might develop school cultures that visually displayed Habits of Mind (HoM); integrated Habits of Mind into all facets of school life by supporting, modeling, monitoring, managing, and engaging in the intentional and deliberate use of the vocabulary of Habits of Mind in all settings. What's more, Fullan (2001) suggested that multiple leadership styles might be heeded when undertaking initiatives to resolve problems, while Green and Swanson (2011), and Senge (1990) agreed that the implementation of instructional programs is often informed by various educational and organizational leadership theories.

Successful implementation of instructional change requires strategic alignment with the overall school vision (Zahn, 2011). For the servant-leader, follow-through on promises to followers is a key strategy of the implementation process (Erkutlu & Chafra, 2015). In essence, a *servant leadership approach*, which encompasses organizational leadership, school visioning, emotional intelligence, and effective communication serves to develop the community for school change.

First coined by Greenleaf (1970), a servant leader is a servant first (What Is Servant Leadership, n.d.). Servant leaders identify themselves as stewards to others and aspire to help them as their main leadership function (Greenleaf, 1977), deriving their authority from service and not power (van Dierendonck & Patterson, 2010). The servant leader shares power by putting others first (What Is Servant Leadership, n.d.) and to influence the vision of the school (Sergiovanni, 2007).

Beyond that, the role of a servant leader is not solely designated to administrators. Servant leaders are "cognizant of the school's big picture while empowering its people to be more, do more, and achieve more by providing emotional support, intellectual growth, and physical resources needed for success" (Brumley, 2012, p. 37). Servant leaders build the leadership capacities of adults and students in the school setting by building teams, sharing decisions and promoting collegiality (Sergiovanni, 1992).

Servant leaders accomplish this focus on empowerment by improving the school for the students, the faculty, and for society at large (Brumley, 2012). Servant leaders as teacher leaders ask values questions, such as "What are we about? Why? Are students being served? Is the school learning as a community being served? What are our obligations to this community? And with these questions in mind, how can we best get the job done?" (Sergiovanni, 1992, pp. 128–129).

Leaders who want to empower others for implementing organizational change must also be teachers (Ford, 1991). Teachers lead students and colleagues daily based on dispositions they have developed rather than due to their positional titles (Hill & Berardelli, 2018). Positioning teachers as leaders, who can actualize their own use of Habits of Mind while simultaneously implementing servant leadership in their personal relationships with their colleagues and students, creates a more thorough implementation of Habits of Mind (Costa & Kallick, 2008).

Teachers who engage in servant leadership (SL) are focused on creating school environments that are meaningful and rewarding for all (Tomlinson, 2017). Collaboration and collective decision making are central to embracing systems-wide change by acknowledging the perspectives of various school personnel, not just the formal leader of a school (Culver, 2009).

The "first among equals" approach relies on shared vision and purpose, rather than formal positions of authority (Sergiovani, 2007, p. 57), thus making servant leadership an exceptional framework for understanding teachers as servant leaders and for exploring how servant leadership supports implementation and change efforts in schools.

The purpose of this chapter is to explain how teachers have and may be able to further leverage the servant leadership and Habit of Mind frameworks to advance needed changes within themselves, their colleagues, learning institutions and most importantly, their students. This chapter depicts examples of teachers' use of servant leadership and Habits of Mind from the literature and two research studies. Examples of teacher use of Habits of Mind through servant leadership provide valid reasons for the broader school community to buy into the importance of Habits of Mind and to create necessary changes.

CONNECTIONS BETWEEN HABITS OF MIND AND SERVANT LEADERSHIP: A NEW CONNECTED FRAMEWORK TO IMPLEMENT HABITS OF MIND

Given their shared conceptual frameworks, Habits of Mind and Servant Leadership work synergistically to support teacher leaders as they accomplish personal and professional goals. Habits of Mind and Servant Leadership are founded on common components of emotional intelligence such as empathy, impulse control, and persistence (Goleman, 1995).

Listening with empathy, metacognition—also known as reflective thinking—remaining open to continuous learning, thinking flexibly, and communicating with clarity and precision are the principal hallmarks of servant leadership and essential Habits of Mind for effective leadership (Costa & Kallick, 2008).

This section introduces the Habits of Mind as they connect with the components of Servant Leadership in the existing literature. Each section also illustrates teacher servant leadership examples from participants who used Habits of Mind and Servant Leadership core concepts in their teacher leader practices with colleagues and students.

Examples are drawn from two current studies on Habits of Mind and leadership (Vazquez, 2020; Vazquez & Piro, 2021). Vazquez's 2020 study involved eight student-participants and eight teacher participants. These participants shared their perceptions of the impact of Habits of Mind on students. Vazquez and Piro's 2021 study included seven teacher-leader participants and focused on the possible ways that these teacher-leaders integrated Habits of Mind into their servant leadership roles, as they led colleagues and/or students.

Habits of Mind/Emotional Intelligence

Emotional intelligence as a product of Habits of Mind is supported by literature in the Servant Leadership framework. Goleman (1995) established that intelligence and emotions are mutually dependent, and his definition of emotional intelligence included empathy, impulse control, persistence, and delayed gratification. Fostering one's ability to manage impulsivity by persisting under difficult circumstances and the ability to demonstrate empathy by listening to others to build understanding are fundamental to fully develop intellect (Costa & Kallick, 2008). Emotional intelligence becomes the product of Habits of Mind that are "cultivated, articulated, operationalized, taught, fostered, modeled and assessed" (Costa & Kallick, 2008, p. 13).

Costa and Kallick's 16 HoM, as dispositions for intelligent behaviors, mirror Servant Leadership's focus on emotional intelligence (EI) in leadership practices. Emotional Intelligence is a core component of Servant Leadership. Servant leaders help followers *mature emotionally, intellectually, and ethically* (Coetzer et al., 2017). EI can be defined as "The subset of social intelligence that involves the ability to monitor one's own and others' feelings and emotions, to discriminate among them and to use this information to guide one's thinking and actions" (Salovey & Meyer, 1990, p. 189).

A relationship between EI and follower perception of SL behaviors has been found (Coetzer, Bussin, & Geldenhuys, 2017). Leaders with high emotional intelligence are effective at managing their own and the emotions of others (Moore, 2009). Servant leaders with high emotional intelligence are apt at developing functional relationships with diverse people and groups (Fullan, 2002). Building level principals' overall emotional intelligence significantly affect standards of leadership performance, such as organization to improve student learning staff efficacy, instructional leadership, and visionary leadership (Cook, 2006).

Participants in the first study (Vazquez, 2020) did not explicitly equate emotional intelligence and Habits of Mind. They perceived them as two distinct initiatives. However, participants in the second study (Vazquez & Piro, 2021) made the connection between emotional intelligence, dispositions and leadership.

For example, one participant stated, "A central tenet of leadership, EQ drives communication. Leaders must not only understand their own feelings and objectives, but the mental state of those they are attempting to lead, and then react appropriately based on that understanding" (Vazquez & Piro, 2021).

A second participant explained, "Emotional intelligence, especially the ability to communicate effectively and empathize with others, is paramount in the teaching profession. In fact, it is perhaps the most important trait(s) that an effective teacher can have" (Vazquez & Piro, 2021). A third participant addressed emotional intelligence as it relates to leadership when she observed, "People with stronger emotional intelligence will foster stronger relationships, trust and greater motivation" (Vazquez & Piro, 2021).

Listening with Empathy and Understanding

Both HoM and Servant Leadership frameworks support listening and more specifically, listening with empathy. The Habit of Mind of Listening with Empathy and Understanding fosters intelligent behavior by facilitating the ability to perceive and appropriately respond to the perspective and emotions of others (Altan, Lane, & Dottin, 2019). Good leaders assist colleagues who are seeking to resolve their own problems, whether they be simple or multi-layered and complex, by listening and with the ultimate goal of understanding and empathy (Costa & Kallick, 2008).

Leaders who are trusted operate as colleagues on a personal level by listening, paraphrasing, and summarizing thereby valuing their relationships with others (Costa & Kallick, 2008). Leaders who are competent and effective in the Habit of Mind of Listening with Empathy and Understanding can focus on their colleague completely, acknowledge the feeling and message that is communicated; are other centered; and demonstrate humanity by responding on a personal level to the immediacy of the situation rather than on how the situation impacts themselves and their positional role (Costa & Kallick, 2008).

Servant leaders communicate well, but first, listen (Parris & Peachey, 2013). Spears and Lawrence (2002) stated that listening included "getting in touch with one's own inner voice and seeking to understand what one's body, spirit and mind are communicating" (p. 5). Greenleaf (1977) suggested that "sustained intentness of listening" (p. 16) is part of the servant leaders' core dispositions.

Both listening and empathy were part of a Servant Leadership Questionnaire, a measure based upon Greenleaf's (1970) and Spears' (1995) characterizations of servant leadership (Coetzer, Bussin, & Geldenhuys, 2017). Listening may be an ethical imperative of servant leadership which suggests opening the heart to others (Reynolds, 2013). As part of identifying the will of the group (Greenleaf, 1970), listening is a fundamental activity of servant leaders in the implementation of Habits of Mind in schools.

Listening with Empathy and Understanding was a fundamental servant leadership disposition which participants in both studies valued seeing in their students and in themselves. A participant attempting to lead students through perspectival listening observed, "Listening with Empathy and Understanding is a Habit of Mind students need to improve upon. Students have a tough time really listening to other points of view and speaking before they have thought" (Vazquez, 2020).

Participants in the second study (Vazquez & Piro, 2021) were able to extrapolate the notion of listening to their own leadership practices. One participant explained that when colleagues were upset about a decision they made, they listened and encouraged brainstorming as a team to provide team input. When discussing helping a colleague through a frustrating experience, a participant stated, "In order for me to best help teachers be successful, I need to understand where they are coming, so that I can predict, plan, and adjust my response, knowing them more personally" (Vazquez & Piro, 2021).

A third participant addressed the specific process he used to become a better servant leader: First, I just listen. Then, I may ask some questions to gain a better understanding of the issue. Finally, I restate their concerns and then we see if we can pinpoint a specific problem we can possibly address or if this is something we cannot control and just need time to process (Vazquez & Piro, 2021).

Participants also identified the need to be a servant leader by listening to students as a HoM disposition. For example, a participant noted that "Listening to student responses in any classroom setting requires empathy and understanding to get to know where they are coming from, not only in their learning in that specific context, but also as humans" (Vazquez & Piro, 2021).

Metacognition/Reflective Thinking

Thinking about thinking (metacognition) is an intelligent behavior which requires that individuals who exercise leadership roles be reflective about their thinking and its impact on others (Altan, Lane, & Dottin, 2019). Metacognition is a self-evaluation of an individual's thoughts and a quintessential component of having an educated mind (Martinez, 2006). Thinking about thinking involves reflecting upon "thoughts, strategies, feelings, and actions and their effects on others.

"Leaders 'talk' to themselves as they evaluate their plans, monitor their progress, and reflect on their actions, needs, and aspirations" (Costa & Kallick, 2008, p. 388). Metacognition functions as a vehicle for deeper learning to occur (Costa & Kallick, 2008; Snyder & Snyder, 2008). Metacognition promotes greater knowledge construction (Cheung & Hew, 2010; Hew & Cheung, 2011). Metacognition is a precursor to all other Habits of Mind (Muscott, 2018). The Habits of Mind function synergistically as clusters of behaviors are implemented in unison to achieve an individual's goals in an intelligent manner (Costa & Kallick, 2008).

Reflective thinking as part of a servant leadership framework mirrors the HoM concept of metacognition. Self-awareness through reflection is critical for leaders. A reflective leader recognizes how change occurs, both within the self and the environment (San Juan & Residence, 2005).

Self-awareness is one of Greenleaf's (1977) attributes of servant leadership. He stated, "Awareness is not a giver of solace–it is just the opposite, it is a disturber and an awakener. Able leaders are usually sharply awake and reasonably disturbed. They are not seekers after solace. They have their own inner serenity" (p. 41).

Reflective thinking and the subsequent generative conversation challenge one's existing mind maps while also stimulating diverse thinking styles (Senge et al., 2012). Additionally, individuals and groups make their thinking, assumptions, and behaviors more visible through meaningful interpersonal interactions (Senge et al., 2012). As part of the implementation process of Habits of Mind, reflective listening on the part of the teacher servant-leader is necessary.

Metacognition and awareness of thinking were identified as key concepts for HoM and leadership by participants. Teacher and student participants agreed that effectively using metacognition successfully required making the time to reflect on one's thought process in order to drive future improvement (Vazquez, 2020). A student participant understood that one needs to stop and pinpoint which Habits of Mind one is using in order to act and respond thoughtfully (Vazquez, 2020). Regarding the use of metacognition when leading colleagues, one participant reflected: It is important for leaders to help those under their charge recognize the thinking behind their decisions—especially in an educational setting. An obvious example is helping teachers define the thinking behind their grading protocols. What is the purpose of grades and how can they be used to facilitate student growth and mastery (Vazquez & Piro, 2021)?

Metacognition and self-awareness of thinking were manifest in participants' interactions with students, as well. A teacher participant noted: We ask the children after almost all of our lessons what they think went well, what they noticed was interesting to them, what they noticed was easy or difficult and why they feel that way. We also ask what they think they need to work on to help improve their learning (Vazquez & Piro, 2021).

Remaining Open to Continuous Learning/Team Learning with Shared Vision

Complacency is the antithesis to the Habit of Mind of Remaining Open to Continuous Learning. Leaders who employ this habit express vulnerability and humility coupled with an intense desire to transcend minimal expectations for those that they serve, and they do not settle for the status quo (Costa & Kallick, 2008).

Leaders who implement the Habit of Mind of Remaining Open to Continuous Learning engage in introspection and self-modify accordingly by reflecting on their experiences and applying what they learn to future activities, tasks, and challenges (Costa & Kallick, 2008). These leaders continuously acknowledge their personal and professional limitations, and they are motivated to improve through their curiosity to find a better way (Costa & Kallick, 2008).

Like the dispositions of remaining open to continuous learning, servant leaders assist followers to remain open to ongoing learning through collaboration and team learning and by relying on a shared vision. Both formal and informal servant leaders develop a shared vision through purpose and community growth and empower others to act and grow as part of that community (Sergiovanni, 2007).

Servant leaders conceive of the school as a learning community where delegation is the key function of the organization (Selznick, 1948). These leaders engage themselves and others in decision-making (Sergiovanni, 2007). It is through the common values of a learning organization that "people continually expand their capacity to create the results they truly desire, where new and expansive patterns of thinking are nurtured, where collective aspiration is set free, and where people are continually learning to see the whole together" (Senge, 1990, p. 3) via remaining open to others.

Participants in both studies noted their use of continuous learning and team learning within their leadership. Teacher participants successfully conveyed to their students the need to remain a continuously improving learner to students. One student remarked, "So often you change your mind on what answer you see, just by hearing other people's opinions and the information they gathered. By *Remaining Open to Continuous Learning* it allows for a change in perspective" (Vazquez, 2020). Regarding continuous learning with colleagues, one participant believed:

> In modeling flexibility and curiosity in all of my work. When I am working with colleagues, I need to be open to new ideas and new perspectives in the moment and model my own learning. It creates a feeling that we are truly colleagues working together for a greater and shared purpose, rather than setting a tone that

I am there to teach them something. The latter only creates division. (Vazquez & Piro, 2021)

Another participant stated how he shared website lessons and a webinar with colleagues. A third addressed continuous learning by emphasizing that all assignments were formative and stating, "The final product is constantly in a state of revision based on students' willingness to create multiple drafts which illustrate the evolution of their thinking and skill acquisition" (Vazquez & Piro, 2021).

THINKING FLEXIBLY AND COMMUNICATING WITH CLARITY AND PRECISION/DEVELOPING A SHARED VISION THROUGH EFFECTIVE COMMUNICATION

Successful leaders can be adaptable by Thinking Flexibly and are able to alter their perspectives and modes of communication thereby generating multiple options and solutions that work for the larger group and serve in the best interest of all (Costa & Kallick, 2008). Leaders who think flexibly can see the perspectives of others and will consider, express and paraphrase the thinking of others in order to evaluate the merits and consequences of multiple courses of action (Costa & Kallick, 2008, p. 181).

Simultaneously, effectual leaders also employ Thinking and Communication with Clarity and Precision by being clear as they express their thinking and further, by monitoring that others have understood them (Costa & Kallick, 2008). Tone, wording timing, pacing and intent are critical components of Communicating with Clarity and Precision and anticipating the need to choose words carefully mitigates resistance, anxiety and enables the listener to hear the message (Costa & Kallick, 2008).

Likewise, communication is a key attribute of servant leadership (Melrose, 1997; Neuschel, 1998) and servant leaders must be able to communicate and develop a shared vision (Melrose, 1997; Ulrich, 1996). In servant leadership, collective visioning promotes communicating with stakeholders with clarity and precision. As part of collective visioning for servant leaders, understanding one's own beliefs and meaning making and interacting with new ways of thinking in concert with others develops shared aspirations (Goleman et al., 2013).

Team learning allows for individuals that form institutions to act in tandem even though their thinking may differ (Senge et al., 2012). By taking personal accountability and capability as core values of servant leaders, shared visions are achieved via effective communication (Parris & Peachey, 2013). Dialogue, listening and speaking with stakeholders is part of this communication strategy. For the servant leader, deep communication gets at the heart of context and meaning making between individuals (Goleman et al., 2013) and a necessary step for implementing Habits of Mind.

Teacher participants in both studies effectively conveyed for their students the benefits of Thinking Flexibly and Communicating with Clarity and Precision as these Habits of Mind contributed to academic success for students who used these Habits of Mind. A teacher described having his students communicate with clarity and precision as the bread and butter of what he did (Vazquez, 2020).

A student voiced the benefit of thinking flexibly in order to succeed and remarked, "Thinking flexibly, because that's good to use, if you have trouble solving a problem. You can have different ways to solve a problem. If you try one way, and it doesn't work out, you can use another way" (Vazquez, 2020). Thinking flexibly and communicating shared visions were also manifest in participants' views of using HoM for leadership.

For one participant in study two (Vazquez & Piro, 2021), leadership meant going in with a plan, thinking and predicting needs, but also, "going in to seek information to adjust as needed."Another participant observed that being collaborative rather than authoritarian allowed flexibility to emerge collaboratively. She added, "I always try to look at a situation in a different way, or from a different perspective and consider all options before making decisions" (Vazquez & Piro, 2021).

Leading students, participants also relied on flexibility. "In my classes, almost everything is flexible: students are encouraged to take unique approaches to literary analysis which is promoted by debate and a collegial exchange of ideas" (Vazquez & Piro, 2021). Communicating with Clarity and Precision also helped teacher leaders to know that their messages were not only heard but understood and this applied to interactions with students and their peers.

One teacher leader voiced, "I also ask for my colleagues to share with me what they think I have said to be sure we are all 'hearing' the same thing" (Vazquez & Piro, 2021). The teacher-leader also took the same approach with students and explained, "I also always allow for questions in case something was missed or I was not as clear as I thought I was" (Vazquez & Piro, 2021).

SUGGESTIONS FOR IMPLEMENTATION AND CONCLUSION

As demonstrated in the framework from the previous section, Habits of Mind are explicitly connected with Servant Leadership principles as evidenced by connections through the literature and through data from two studies on Habits of Mind and leadership. It is reasonable to suggest that Servant Leadership practices and Habits of Mind are inextricably united and therefore, we posit ways that this framework may be implemented for needed change.

First, teachers may consider learning and practicing Habits of Mind with their students and with their colleagues so that they are able to use them with fluency and ease. Using Habits of Mind may further their students' learning success and teachers' own professional success as teacher servant-leaders in the classroom, school and the district.

Teachers may also consider reflecting upon where opportunities to use Habits of Mind and servant leadership show up in their professional and personal lives so that Habits of Mind as they relate with servant leadership are not viewed as something to do, but rather as *a way to be.*

Further, teachers may regularly document the benefits of Habits of Mind as they employ servant leadership practices with their students and with their colleagues. This documentation might be done via Zoom recordings or informal journaling. Self or colleague feedback and/or coaching might be provided through applications such as Mote, in Google Forms or voice over internet protocols (VoIP) such as Zoom. Sharing these reflective anecdotes with administration and colleagues can further help in the implementation of these best practices.

Analogously, teachers may lead professional development sessions on their use of specific Habits of Mind related to servant leadership and the positive impact these habits have on student learning and improved collaboration with colleagues. Finally, teachers may also consider publishing their use of Habits of Mind via servant leadership experiences in educational journals, podcasts, and blogs.

Habits of Mind and Servant Leadership are more than just another effort for school improvement. The problems students and educators are currently encountering cannot be resolved through easily accessible answers, they are complicated and often paradoxical, requiring the use of thinking dispositions and a servant-leadership mindset that recognize opportunities to share vision and processes with others.

The use of Habits of Mind and Servant Leadership as a connected framework, as we have provided in this chapter, present key opportunities for students to succeed. Habits of Mind and Servant Leadership are ways of being that exemplify the highest dispositions for thinking and behavior, both for the individual and for the learning organization.

While school administration may support teachers to further learn and use Habits of Mind and Servant leadership dispositions and practices, it is the teacher servant-leader who transfers these dispositions and behaviors into the classroom and implements them in their roles as leaders.

Just as students learn that Habits of Mind have applicable transfer among various subjects and in their personal lives, teachers may consider thinking about the ubiquitous nature of the connections between Habits of Mind and Servant Leadership to improve the lives of their students, their own, and those of the colleagues they lead.

SUMMARY

This chapter illustrated the connections between servant teacher leaders and Habits of Mind for student success through the literature and through data from two studies on Habits of Mind and leadership. Servant Leadership and Habits of Mind work synergistically through the common components of emotional intelligence, listening with empathy, metacognition, remaining open to continuous learning, thinking flexibly, and communicating with clarity and precision.

REFERENCES

Altan, S., Lane, J. F., & Dottin, E. (2019). Using habits of mind, intelligent behaviors, and educational theories to create a conceptual framework for developing effective teaching dispositions. *Journal of Teacher Education, 70*(2), 169–183. doi: 10.1177/0022487117736024

Brumley, C. (2012). *Leadership standards in action: The school principal as servant-leader.* Rowman & Littlefield Education.

Cheung, W. S., & Hew, K. F. (2010). Examining facilitators' habits of mind in an asynchronous online discussion environment: A two cases study. *Australasian Journal of Educational Technology, 26*(1). doi: 10.14742/ajet.1106

Coetzer, M. F., Bussin, M., & Geldenhuys, M. (2017). The functions of a servant leader. *Administrative Sciences (2076–3387), 7*(1), 1–32. doi:10.3390/admsci7010005

Cook, C. R. (2006). *Effects of emotional intelligence on principals' leadership performance.* Montana State University. https://scholarworks.montana.edu/xmlui/bitstream/ handle/1/1099/ cookc0506 .pdf? sequence=1&sa=U&ei=z2xSU7zCFO fU8AGh4ICoAg& ved =0CEQQFjAH&usg=AFQjCNFB_JLMQE7_POr9AdhoJ xwpu4FwsQ

Costa, A. L., & Kallick, B. (2008). *Learning and leading with habits of mind: 16 essential characteristics for success.* Alexandria, VA: Association for Supervision and Curriculum Development.

Culver, M. K. (2009). *Applying servant leadership in today's schools.* Eye On Education.

Darling-Hammond, L., Bullmaster, M. L., & Cobb, V. L. (1995). Rethinking teacher leadership through professional development schools. *Elementary School Journal, 96*, 87–106.

Erkutlu, H., & Chafra, J. (2015). The effects of empowerment role identity and creative role identity on servant leadership and employees' innovation implementation behavior. *Procedia-Social and Behavioral Sciences, 181*, 3–11.

Fiarman, S. E. (2017). *Building a schoolwide leadership mindset.* https://www.ascd.org/el/articles/building-a-schoolwide-leadership-mindset

Ford, L. (1991). *Transforming leadership: Jesus' way of creating vision, shaping values, an empowering change.* Downers Grove, IL: InterVarsity Press.

Fullan, M. (2001). *Leading in a culture of change.* Hoboken, NH: Jossey-Bass, a Wiley brand.

Fullan, M. (2002). Principals as leaders in a culture of change. *Educational Leadership, Special Issue*, May 2002.

Goleman, D. (1995). *Emotional intelligence.* New York, NY: Bantam Books.

Goleman, D., Boyatzis, R. E., & McKee, A. (2013). *Primal leadership: Realizing the power of emotional intelligence.* Boston, MA: Harvard Business School Press.

Gordon, M. (2011). Mathematical habits of mind: Promoting students' thoughtful considerations. *Journal of Curriculum Studies, 43*(4), 457–469. doi: 10.1080/00220272.2011.578664

Greenleaf, R. K. (1970). *The servant as leader.* Robert K. Greenleaf Publishing Center.

Greenleaf, R. K. (1977). *Servant leadership: A journey into the nature of legitimate power and greatness.* Mahwah, NJ: Paulist Press.

Green, J., & Swanson, T. (2011). Tightening the system: Reference as a loosely coupled system. *Journal of Library Administration, 51*(4), 375–388. doi:10.1080/01930826.2011.556960

Hew, K. F., & Cheung, W. S. (2011). Student facilitators' habits of mind and their influences on higher-level knowledge construction occurrences in online discussions: a case study. *Innovations in Education and Teaching International, 48*(3), 275–285. doi: 10.1080/14703297.2011.593704

Hill, M., & Berardelli, P. (October 3, 2018). *Walk this Way.* Retrieved November 15, 2021, from https://www.ascd.org/blogs/walk-this-way.

Kay, K., & Greenhill, V. (2012). *The education leaders guide: 7 steps toward 21st century schools and districts.* Boston, MA: Allyn & Bacon.

Martinez, M. E. (2006). What is metacognition? *Phi Delta Kappan*, 696–699. doi: 10.1177/003172170608700916

Melrose, K. (1997). Putting servant leadership into practice. In L. C. Spears, (Ed.), *Insights on leadership: Service, stewardship, spirit, and servant-leadership.* New York, NY: John Wiley.

Moore, B. (2009). Emotional intelligence for school administrators: A priority for school reform? *American Secondary Education, 37*(3), 20–28.

Muscott, P. G. (2018) *Habits of mind and performance task achievement* (Unpublished Master's Thesis). London: University of Roehampton.

Neuschel, R. P. (1998). *The servant-leader: Unleashing the power of your people.* East Lansing, MI: Vision Sports Management.

Parris, D., & Peachey, J. (2013). A systematic literature review of servant leadership theory in organizational contexts. *Journal of Business Ethics, 113*(3), 377.

Reynolds, K. (January 2013). Listening: An ethical imperative for servant-leaders. In *Servant-leadership: Practice and application.: Selected proceedings of the Pacific Northwest Regional Servant Leadership Conference* (pp. 117–130). Marylhurst University Center for Servant Leadership.

Salovey, P., & Mayer, J. D. (1990). Emotional intelligence. *Imagination, cognition and personality, 9*(3), 185–211.

San Juan, K. S., & Residence, J. J. (2005). Re-imagining power in leadership: Reflection, integration and servant-leadership. *International Journal of Servant Leadership, 1*(1), 187–212.

Selznick, P. (1948). Foundations of the theory of organization. *American Sociological Review, 13*(1), 25–35.

Senge, P. M. (1990). *The fifth discipline: The art and practice of the learning organization.* New York: Doubleday/Currency.

Senge, P. (2000). Classic work: The leader's new work: Building learning organizations. In D. Morey, M. T. Maybury, & B. M. Thuraisingham (Eds.), *Knowledge management: Classic and contemporary works.* (pp. 19–52). Cambridge, MA: MIT Press.

Senge, P. M. (2012). Creating schools for the future, not the past for all students. *Leader to Leader,* (65), 44–49. doi:10.1002/ltl.20035

Sergiovanni, T. J. (1992). *Moral leadership: Getting to the heart of school improvement.* San Francisco: Jossey-Bass Publishers.

Sergiovanni, T. J. (2007). *Rethinking leadership: A collection of articles.* Corwin Press.

Snyder, L. G., & Snyder, M. J. (2008). Teaching critical thinking and problem solving skills. *The Delta Pi Epsilon Journal, L*(2), 90–99.

Spears, L. (1995). Servant-leadership and the Greenleaf legacy. In L. Spears (Ed.), *Reflections on leadership: How Robert K. Greenleaf's theory of servant leadership influenced today's top management thinkers.* New York: J. Wiley.

Spears, L. C., & Lawrence, M. (Eds.). (2002). *Focus on leadership: Servant-leadership for the twenty-first century.* John Wiley & Sons.

Tomlinson, C. A. (2017). *Shining a Light on Leadership—Educational Leadership.* http://www.ascd.org/publications/educational-leadership/may17/vol74/num08/Shining-a-Light-on-Leadership.aspx

Ulrich, D. (1996). Credibility X Capability. In F. Hesselbein, M. Goldsmith, & R. Beckhard (Eds.), *The leader of the future: New visions, strategies and practices for the next era* (pp. 209–219). Essay, Jossey-Bass Publishers.

van Dierendonck, D., & Patterson, K. (2010). *Servant leadership: Developments in theory and research.* Palgrave Macmillan, UK.

Vazquez, J. C. (2020). *The impact of Habits of Mind: An exploratory study,*[Doctoral dissertation, Western Connecticut State University]. Western Connecticut State

University Education Dissertations. https://westcollections.wcsu.edu /handle/20.500. 12945/199

Vazquez, J. C., & Piro, J. S. (2021). *Teacher perceptions on Habits of Mind and Servant Leadership.* [Unpublished manuscript]. Western Connecticut State University.

What is servant leadership? (n.d.) Retrieved from https://www.greenleaf.org/what-is -servant-leadership/

Zahn, B. (2011). *Elementary teacher assessments of principal servant leadership, their experience with team learning and student academic achievement* [Ed.D., Dowling College].

Chapter 8

Curricular and Content Connections to the Habits of Mind

Creating Stickiness with the Habits

Nick Bruski

In an educational landscape of rigorous Common Core Standards, NGSS, new curricular adoptions, mindfulness, social emotional learning, and a never-ending stream of local initiatives, one might ask, "Where do I find time to teach Habits of Mind, and how am I going to get to all 16 of them with meaning, rigor, and transfer?" Is 16 habits too many? The simple answer is yes, 16 habits is too many to explicitly teach over a year. So, what habits do you ditch? None . . . Let me explain.

At our elementary school in Southern California, we worked hard to put the Habits of Mind into place in our classrooms. We wanted to institutionalize them. We wanted them to live within our walls. We did this through a very uncreative and linear approach. To oversimplify, we have 180 days of school and 16 Habits, so basic mathematics says we can spend 11.25 days on each habit. It was great! We "taught" every habit equally and checked all 16 boxes.

Unfortunately, the result was lifeless and uninspired lip-service to the great work of Costa and Kallick. Students could match up a habit with its definition, but didn't truly know them, understand them, use them, and live them. To teach for deep understanding that allows students to transfer and apply this knowledge within their own lives, schools need to reflect and design an integrated curriculum that makes the learning stick.

THE SCIENCE OF STICKINESS

Teachers have long been frustrated with students failing to retain and apply what has been taught or "covered" in the classroom. Imagine teaching first grade students four lessons on starting each sentence with a capital letter, observing them successfully correct uncapitalized initial words on multiple worksheets, and then witness more than half the class not use capitals in their writing journals at the end of the week.

Although teachers often have great instincts to improve retention and transfer, there is a large body of research in cognitive neuroscience that illuminates strategies to help learning stick (Inglis, 2015a). In this chapter, we will explore four specific strategies described by Inglis to help students fully understand, retain, and apply the Habits of Mind across the curriculum:

1. Connecting learning to prior knowledge
2. Demonstrating relevance and creating interest
3. Building upon emotional memories
4. Repeating core messages

Connecting Learning to Prior Knowledge

Scenario: A kindergarten teacher is frustrated with her students' writing stamina and ability to edit their work. Being so young and new to their roles as students, she sees a connection and opportunity to connect to the habit of Persistence. She decides that these young 5-year-olds need explicit instruction of what persistence is! The students read and discussed titles like The Little Engine That Could *and* The Digging-est Dog *by Al Perkins. Students then created stick figures and created a bulletin board titled "Sticking with It" with word-bubbles of student-created sentiments and understandings of the importance of curriculum.*

The Habits of Mind should be taught just like one teaches math or reading; in the context of the bigger picture and in connection with content. When the kindergarten students noted above were explicitly taught about persistence through the context of stories, they were then given a reason to understand persistence by applying it to their writing. Students set goals for writing stamina (in terms of minutes) and with the help of the teacher, created their own editing rubric.

In a short period of time, this teacher moved her class from a place where writing lacked capitals, spaces, periods, and even critical letter sounds to one where all but one student met the rubric requirements with 100 percent accuracy. Students moved from staying on task for 5–10 minutes and never revisiting a piece of writing for editing, to working for 20–30 minutes repeatedly on the same project. Not only did she teach her students basic writing skills, but she taught them to persist across the curriculum and in life.

Teachers have long known about the power of connecting learning to prior knowledge. In Madeline Hunter's classic seven-step lesson design taught in many teacher preparation programs, young teachers are asked to design an "anticipatory set" at the beginning of each lesson, designed to spark interest and connect the upcoming lesson to prior learning. According to Inglis (2015a), "When new information is presented, the brain begins its task of seeking patterns within previously encoded information or experiences. In fact, it seems that our brains prefer to use patterns already established rather than to build new patterns."

The brain naturally seeks patterns and looks to fit new ideas into existing frameworks and constructs of understanding. Attaching learning about the Habits of Mind to prior knowledge builds deeper meaning by fitting this "new" material into already existing patterns.

One of the simplest ways to connect learning around the Habits of Mind with prior knowledge is through the use of stories. As described earlier in this chapter, kindergarten students familiar with *The Little Engine That Could* had a simple understanding of a story where a small train tried really hard to get up a hill. This background knowledge provided the base upon which the more complex idea of persistence can be fuller understood and drawn out.

Once you learn to look at children's literature through the lens of the Habits of Mind, many habits will begin to jump out at you. Whether it is within picture books in the younger grades or core literature in the upper grades, books are always written around themes and the interplay between characters creates opportunities to find examples of the Habits of Mind in action.

Demonstrating Meaning and Creating Relevance

Learning sticks when ideas are connected to meaning and the relevance of the power of the Habits of Mind becomes visible. If a child is taught to divide fractions with the standard algorithm in isolation on a worksheet, most likely they will remember how to get the "right" answer for a short while ("Mine is not to question why, just invert and multiply"), but see little value in the task, and more importantly, fail to see the bigger picture of broader mathematical conceptual understandings that could transcend division of fractions and build upon meta-understandings like equal parts, connections to the real world, and more.

Thinking about "stickiness," if the division of fractions is taught through a real-world meaningful context, the learning sticks, students have a reason to learn, and connections can be made to other areas not only in mathematics but across the curriculum. Imagine if your class is raising money for its annual field trip by making and selling school headbands. Each headband takes three-eighths of a yard to make and the class has 23 ¼ yards of material. How many headbands can they make? Just as this task creates relevance and meaning to the area of mathematics, so too must instruction around the Habits of Mind.

"We do not pay attention to things that are boring because our brains are wired to pay attention to things that surprise us, intrigue us, tickle our synapses with novelty, or draw our interest as a prehistoric survival technique" (Inglis, 2015b). Students may be surprised to learn that Michael Jordan, arguably the greatest basketball player of all time, did not make his high school varsity team at his first tryout. By connecting the Habit of persistence to his success, students are shown the relevance of this Habit and how it can have meaning in their own life. His work ethic and motivation to practice harder than everyone else resulted in his success.

By telling the story of Helen Keller becoming deaf and blind at nineteen months, students can see the power of gathering data through all of their senses. A woman who could not hear or see went on to graduate from Radcliffe College at Harvard University, write fourteen books, became a prolific civil rights activist and even had a movie made about her life.

In addition to creating relevance and sparking curiosity about individuals, connections can also be made to organizations and groups of people. How can the success of Apple be explained if not through a company willing to create, imagine and innovate? Apple innovates not only in their products, but also within their internal structures and systems, creating workgroups designed for deep collaboration and sharing of ideas across fields of expertise.

A recent study (AMA, 2019) showed that approximately 35 percent of entrepreneurs in the United States are dyslexic and are known to have strengths in oral communications (thinking and communicating with clarity and precision) and problem solving. The Yale Center for Dyslexia and Creativity (2017) cites, "the power of the dyslexic mind to navigate around obstacles, come up with creative solutions and serve our society in meaningful ways" which serves as a surprising example for students to know that dyslexia, which might be seen as a barrier to success, can actually empower and advantage individuals through their pronounced abilities in specific habits.

Further examples are countless, and teachers should be encouraged to use their own creativity and imagination in finding other connections that demonstrate meaning and create relevance for the Habits of Mind. Is there an underdog sports story where thinking interdependently lead to victory? How critical is striving for accuracy and precision when coding the students' favorite video game?

Teachers themselves should look for stories within their own lives that might surprise their students and demonstrate a real-world example of the Habits' power in their own lives. By finding surprising and interesting connections to the Habits of Mind, teachers create relevance and further demonstrate the meaning of the Habits.

Building Upon Emotional Memories

Strong emotions create strong memories. Because the Habits of Mind are intrinsically personal, there is great opportunity to build strong emotional connections to the Habits of Mind. "The effective use of emotional connections helps to establish relevance, helps students to care and be emotionally invested in the content and the learning experience, which in turn can motivate action" (Inglis, 2015b).

One of the quickest and most effective ways that students can connect with the Habits of Mind is by asking them to think about a time when they have successfully or unsuccessfully used a specific Habit of Mind and reflect upon how that felt. Drawing upon that emotional memory will help to connect that experience to a Habit of Mind and motivate further action.

One of the most obvious emotional connections to the Habits of Mind for students is with Persistence. Everyone has a story about working hard at something. It could be in an academic area like reading or math, or a specific skill in their favorite sport (making a sports team, getting better at free throws, or nailing a backflip). Many students these days can connect to a specific achievement in a video game, or even a number of "likes" on a social media account.

The key here is asking students to remember how it felt to meet their goal and then reflect upon all of the failures and hard work that lead up to it. By bringing back the emotional memories, students are more likely to remember what the habit of persistence means and utilize that habit in the future. They have "re-learned" the lesson by reliving the memory are likely to seek out that feeling once more. Whether learning a significant life lesson or applying the Habits to small moments throughout the day, there are countless opportunities to connect the Habits of Mind to emotions. Below are a few ideas to ignite further exploration into this area.

- *Persisting.* Compare the effort needed for a simple word search with finding Waldo in a *Where's Waldo* puzzle. Ask students which task was more satisfying and why.
- *Listening with Understanding and Empathy.* Ask students about a time when someone really listened to them and understood how they felt.

How did this make them feel? What did that person do to show that they really listened?

- *Managing Impulsivity.* Ask students to reflect on a time when they had to be very patient and resist strong impulses, such as opening up birthday or holiday presents, grabbing candy from a help-yourself Halloween dish, etc.
- *Taking Responsible Risks.* Ask students to think about a time when they tried something new and scary. How did it feel to take a risk? How did it feel after?
- *Finding Humor.* Ask students to think about an embarrassing situation they have had. Were they able to laugh off the embarrassment? How might it feel if they did or could?
- *Thinking Interdependently.* Ask students to think about a time where teamwork lead to a better result. How did it feel to work together as a team?
- *Thinking and Communicating with Clarity and Precision.* Ask students to think about a time when they really wanted someone to understand them, but they just could not get their message across. How did it feel when they were not understood? What could they have done differently?

Repeating Core Messages: Making the Habits of Mind Ubiquitous in Your Curriculum and Environment

As explained in the introduction, just "covering" the Habits is not enough. When the Habits of Mind are infused into both the curriculum and the physical environment of your campus, your community can become fluent in the integration and use of them.

In Michael Schmoker's book *Focus* (2018) he shares that, "There is too much overload and baggage on the current change journey. The skinny is about finding the smallest number of high-leverage, easy-to-understand actions that unleash stunningly powerful consequences." Inglis (2015b) expands on this, stating that the core message, "must be thick, relevant, valuable, and multilayered so that it is not easily dismissed. It should ignite a curiosity to learn more. Once you have a core message, you need to magnify its stickiness by making it visual."

Schools and teachers need to "slow down" and make the Habits their own by examining their core beliefs, values, and unique culture.

Scenario: An elementary school in Southern California identified five habits that they focused on deeply: Thinking Flexibly, Persistence, Listening with Understanding and Empathy, Taking Responsible Risks, and Managing Impulsivity. They became connoisseurs of these five habits and infused them into everything they did. They explicitly taught them in classroom lessons and whole-school assemblies. They sought out connections to literature, characters, historical figures, and various content areas. They opened up staff PLCs with a focus habit, asking the adults to model empathy as they worked through tough inter-staff conflict.

They thought flexibly when met with unanticipated challenges, like the flooding of one of their buildings. They discussed persistence with students in their math classrooms, as students took on rich, open-ended, problem-solving situations. They asked students to show empathy with their peers when issues arose on the playground.

The Habits became a common language on their campus, and by developing fluency in five, they started to naturally see them everywhere, in everything they did, and in what the students did too. They would talk about the persistence they used to finish an assigned reading before a deadline. They could be overheard on the playground encouraging a reluctant friend to take a responsible risk and join a game they had not tried before. It became common to receive an email from a parent, sharing that while at the dinner table, their 6-year-old daughter told them they need to manage their impulsivity as they reached for a second helping of dessert.

As this school built fluency with the initial five, it was clear how ubiquitous these Habits had become, and how powerful they were for students and staff to have in their tool kits. The Habits became a lens to understand the world around them, and to empower them to live fuller and more meaningful lives, both as students, and as human beings. With the success of the original five, the staff and students were naturally curious to explore the other eleven.

When the Habits of Mind become pervasive across all areas of the curricula, as well as the social environment, they do not require traditional "teaching." Even with starting small and primarily focusing on an original five, K-6 schools have seven years with their students, and thousands of opportunities to connect what they do to all 16 Habits of Mind in the course of their tenure at a school. By simplifying one's approach, schools and teachers can learn to do more with the Habits, and use them meaningfully. Schools can and should teach all sixteen, but not in one year and not all at once, so that it no longer *feels* like teaching.

CREATING A SYMBOLIC HEART FOR THE HABITS OF MIND ON YOUR CAMPUS

Ron Ritchhart of Harvard University says that everything you do sends messages about what you value (Tui Boyes, 2019). As schools and teachers begin to think about the Habits of Mind and their environment, a community should ask itself, "What messages are we sending?" and "What messages do we want to send?" Schools seeking to meaningfully incorporate the Habits of Mind into their school environment should consider developing a symbolic center or touchstone for the Habits somewhere on campus. In choosing a location and design, consider the following questions:

- What messages are we sending by choosing this location/design?
- What metaphorical connections might we make?
- What connections to existing curricula, beliefs, or other school symbols might we make?
- Is there an entryway or path where the Habits could be painted on individual steps?

Students could connect to their own developing fluency in the Habits as they walk up into the school at the start of each day. Is there a path where stones could be labeled to represent each habit and symbolize the path students are on in their journey toward developing the Habits? Are there pillars in your hallway that could represent the Habits and symbolize the foundation to becoming successful human beings? Are there trees in a garden that can be named and grow each year, just as one's understanding of the Habits does? The list could go on and on.

At Montecito Union School in Southern California, students worked together with a local artist and parent, Jeremy Harper, to create a large mural in the center of campus dedicated to the Habits of Mind. It is a colorful landscape of local flora and fauna, with a large tree at the center. Hidden within the trunk of the tree is a depiction of Rodin's *The Thinker*, representing the consciousness and critical thinking we want our students to have with the Habits of Mind.

The scene has sixteen waterfalls, one for each Habit, and their names are also incorporated and spread throughout the scene. As students walk toward the mural, actual trees in the foreground frame the mural, creating a real canopy that brings the mural to life. It is a constant reminder that the Habits live on our campus and are a part of everything they do. The mural is located at the very end of a highly traveled pathway near the lunch tables. This location ensures it is seen regularly. Its proximity to the lunch tables also sets the stage for reflection in one of our most communal areas as students eat lunch each day.

Having a symbolic center for the campus sends a message to students, staff and families that the work of the Habits of Mind is an important piece of what you do as a school. Habits only become habits with regular exposure, practice and focus. Having a visual reminder on your campus will help the

Habits live on your campus, bringing them to the regular attention of your entire community.

CONSISTENT VISIBILITY AND EXPOSURE OUTSIDE THE CLASSROOM

In addition to having a symbolic center for the Habits of Mind on campus, there are countless opportunities to reinforce the Habits by seeking further opportunities and connections in the physical environment. By walking one's campus and asking the question, "What messages are we sending with what is displayed on our walls?" opportunities for repeating the core message can be found. If a prospective parent were to tour the school in silence without students, what would they infer by what they see?

Below is a list of ideas to spark your creativity and think about connections and opportunities available on your campus:

- Create a display honoring select students for "Taking Responsible Risks" in making new friendships, participating more in class, and so on.
- Design signage for reminders of expectations, such as Managing Impulsivity when walking quietly by the kindergarten classrooms, or "Listening with Understanding and Empathy" to encourage friendships at the lunch tables.
- Label art displays with "Creating, Imagining, and Innovating."
- Print and frame key quotes connecting to the Habits and hang them in the main office for visitors to reflect on as they enter the school. See the link for examples: (http://www.habitsofmindinstitute.org/resources /quotes/).
- Set out sandwich boards around campus with focused Habits of the week or month.
- Celebrate Spelling Bee Winners with a "Striving for Accuracy" display in the front hall.
- Include the language of the Habits of Mind in student rubrics and self assessments ("*I strove for accuracy and precision when editing my writing for proper nouns and quotation marks*").

The Habits of Mind are incredibly broad and complex, and once a school is in the *habit*, the community will begin to see the Habits in everything they do. As the connections are explicitly labeled and made visible, the entire community will continue to build their own understanding of the Habits. When the Habits of Mind live on a campus, it won't be long before students, families and faculty alike naturally and spontaneously reference them. They become more adept at making sense of the world around them through this lens.

Everything a school does sends messages about what it values. Ask any teacher or administrator and they will let you know that wall space and signage are precious real estate. If a school dedicates one bulletin board to the Habits of Mind in a back hallway near the teachers lounge, how will students and parents know it is important? More than merely paying lip service to the Habits, a school must ensure the Habits are featured prominently across campus and in classrooms in a variety of ways. Get creative with it. Involve students and parents. They will create, imagine, and innovate in ways that will astound you and bring your core message to life.

SUMMARY

One of the most powerful aspects of the Habits of Mind is that they transcend any particular content area. In math, there are clear connections with striving for accuracy, thinking and communicating with clarity and precision, and applying past knowledge to new situations. In literature, understanding character traits is a simple task when seen through the Habits of Mind. Did the characters in the story show persistence? Empathy? Flexible thinking? In social studies, historical figures can be analyzed, and students can be asked to persuade their audience which habits lead to, or hindered, their success!

Regardless of any content area, when teachers become fluent with the Habits of Mind, they seek and find opportunities to fluidly and meaningfully connect the Habits to what they are already doing. This teaching in context gives meaning to the Habits while also working to develop a deep and intrinsic understanding of them. Furthermore, it supports a more rigorous and complex understanding of the content! As a community becomes more and more entrenched in the Habits of Mind, even students will begin to notice connections and name Habits in places one may never have expected, making the learning stick.

REFERENCES

AMA Staff. (January 24, 2019). *New research reveals many entrepreneurs are dyslexic*. AMA. Retrieved December 26, 2021, from https://www.amanet.org/articles/new-research-reveals-many-entrepreneurs-are-dyslexic/
Inglis, A. H. (March 25, 2015). *Stick, stick, stick: Teaching for sticky learning—part 1—Seminarium: A blog community created by Religious Studies and seminary*

educators. Seminarium. Retrieved December 26, 2021, from http://seminariumblog .org/general/semclass/stick-stick-stick-teaching-sticky-learning-part-1/

Inglis, A. H. (March 27, 2015). *YOU CAN'T FISH WITHOUT BAIT: Teaching for sticky learning—Part 2—Seminarium: A blog community created by Religious Studies and seminary educators*. Seminarium. Retrieved December 26, 2021, from http://seminariumblog.org/general/semclass/you-cant-fish-without-bait-teaching -for-sticky-learning-part-2/

Schmoker, M. J. (2018). *Focus: Elevating the essentials to radically improve student learning*. ASCD.

Tui Boyes, K. (March 29, 2019). *Using the classroom space to promote thinking and learning*. LinkedIn. Retrieved December 27, 2021, from https://www.linkedin.com /pulse/using-classroom-space-promote-thinking-learning-karen-tui-boyes-csp

Yale Center for Dyslexia and Creativity. (2017). *Success stories*. Yale Dyslexia. Retrieved December 26, 2021, from https://dyslexia.yale.edu/success-stories/ ?sscat=artists-architects-designers

Chapter 9

A Guaranteed, Intentional Curriculum Focused on Thinking Dispositions

Philip G. Muscott

Much has been said in this book regarding the need for both educators and students to cultivate cognitive strategies for self-directed and lifelong learning. It is time to turn our attention to practical ways in which we can thoughtfully and intentionally design curriculum to enable students to attain these lofty goals.

Many educators and curriculum theorists state that when designing curriculum, the more clearly the desired results are stated, the higher the likelihood that the students will reach these goals (Barendregt et al., 2016; Krajcik et al., 2008; White, 2007). It stands to reason cognitive dispositions, notably the 16 Habits of Mind, should likewise be stated clearly.

When educators use sets of academic standards or state-set targets to drive curriculum and lesson planning, the thinking dispositions needed for students to attain these mandated results and apply them to real-world situations are often missing. This chapter illustrates how the *Understanding by Design* framework (UbD; Wiggins & McTighe, 2005) can help curriculum designers in any field state learning goals clearly and include both cognitive and affective aspects of learning.

By using the UbD template and tools, this chapter clearly explains and describes how HoM as goals can be achieved by students. These templates found in Tables 9.1 and 9.2 can be used as a reference while reading the supplemental information provided below. This unit plan was designed for schools where students are challenged to explore a wide variety of topics, many of them controversial.

Table 9.1. Desired Results

Stage 1: Learning Goals	
Established Goals	*Long-Term Transfer Goals*
Habits of Mind Competency Standards *Managing impulsivity: 8* Meaning *(2.8.M)* Know that employing Managing Impulsivity strategies can often lead to hidden and deeper meaning making than jumping to quick conclusions on a topic or viewpoint. Capacity *(2.8.Ca)* Skilled at avoiding hasty judgement on complex issues and viewpoints by employing close reading and listening strategies. Commitment *(2.8.Co)* Set specific goals to improve their listening and reading strategies, in order to avoid jumping to hasty conclusions and judgements on complex topics. *Responding with wonderment and awe: 8* Meaning *(12.9.M)* Students will know that Responding with Wonderment and Awe can be a catalyst for further investigation into topics, and the creation of solutions to societal issues? Capacity *(12.9.Ca)* skilled at finding aspects of Wonderment and Awe in the world around them in order to inspire action. Commitment *(12.9.Co)* Students will set specific goals in an attempt to see the Wonderment and Awe in the world around them, which in turn may lead to engagement in certain causes or campaigns.	*What kinds of long-term, independent accomplishments are desired? Students will be able to independently use their learning to . . .* T1 Critically appraise information for validity and reliability in order to aid decision making and potential modification of personal worldview. T2 Make informed decisions after analyzing situations from multiple perspectives. T3 Effectively handle conflicts and misunderstanding through the use of empathy.

The unit is on religion in Grade 8 in an international school in Phnom Penh, Cambodia. The school's curriculum framework includes academic standards from the United States, utilizes UbD for curriculum planning, infuses all units with a selection of the HoM, and is accredited by ACS WASC.

The topic of religion is sensitive and emotive; varying and differing beliefs may result in minor disagreements but can also lead to horrific and deadly

Table 9.2. Desired Results

Stage 1: Learning Goals	
Meaning	
Understanding(s)	*Essential Question(s)*
What specifically do you want students to understand? What inferences should they make? Students will understand that . . . U1 Students will understand that individuals and institutions can respond to conflict in a range of ways, including aggression, diplomacy, indifference, or avoidance. The choice of approach is influenced by a range of factors, including, but not limited to, ideology, culture, economic gain, and the origins and time frame of the conflict. U2 Students will understand that religion has an impact on the world, with varying significance to individuals and influence over the way people live. It can range from shaping personal perspective on ethics and morals to being a catalyst of conflict around the world.	What thought-provoking questions will foster inquiry, meaning making, and transfer? Students will keep considering . . . Q1 How can we effectively handle conflict and misunderstanding? Q2 Is religion a force for good in the world?
Acquisition	
Knowledge	*Skill(s)*
What facts and basic concepts should students know and be able to recall? Students will know . . . K1 Key terms: Monotheism, polytheism, atheism, theology, theocracy, Sharia Law, 5 pillars of Islami Mecca, Medina, mosque. K2 The origins and basic tenets of some of the world's major religions, including Islam. K3 The workings of religious texts, including the differences between the Quaran and the Hadith. K4 Examples of religious discrimination including the Rohingya discrimination in Myanmar. K5 Cause and effects of religious conflicts including the Sunni Shiite conflict in the Muslim world.	What discrete skills and processes should students be able to use? Students will be skilled at . . . S1 Evidence: Students can support their claims with evidence, including primary source quotations S2 Perspective-taking: Students can identify, explain, and assess different perspectives on an issue S3 Conflict Resolution

wars. Students need cultural awareness and sensitivity to understand and respect these differences. The Institute for Habits of Mind (2021) advocates that it is important to educate students for a more thoughtful world; therefore, students need cognitive skills to constructively debate, discuss, and engage in civil discourse.

While debating, discussing, and engaging involves the wherewithal to support and defend their beliefs, values, and viewpoints, it also requires the ability to be open-minded and think flexibly. The templates and tools from the UbD framework help illustrate how HoM-related goals, assessment standards, and learning strategies can address controversial issues such as religion in the classroom.

The template features an example of how students can explore the history, details, and messages of an excerpt from one religious text, the Old Testament. By using Habits of Mind to design curriculum about controversial issues such as religion, students can learn to employ more empathy toward different groups, view situations from multiple perspectives, and think more flexibly when formulating solutions to the complex problems surrounding these issues.

Following the description and discussion of the UbD example and model, the chapter explains with how this unit can be combined others. In particular, it discusses how tools of UbD can be used to "map" how HoM are addressed in the curriculum.

ARTICULATING DESIRED RESULTS

One of the strengths of the UbD framework is that in Stage 1 (Desired Results), the goals of the unit are broken down into the following elements: Knowledge (declarative), Skills (procedural), Understandings (conceptual) and Transfer (one's ability to put all of the learning together, and apply it to new concepts; McTighe, 2014). This chapter argues that an additional section to the desired results, cognitive dispositions or HoM, are essential for students to attain the goals of the unit, especially Transfer.

Using UbD in combination with HoM helps parse out the various meanings of each of the Habits. For example, the HoM *Thinking Interdependently* can be related to Collaboration, an essential "21st Century Skill" (Partnership for 21st Century Skills, 2008; Rotherham & Willingham, 2010; Voogt & Roblin, 2010).

But do we mean when we say we want students to collaborate? In addition, how can we expect students to know *how* to work interdependently unless it is made explicit in our planning and instruction? Something as seemingly obvious as collaborative decision making is not as clear-cut as it may first appear. What strategies do we wish our students to know, be alert to, apply, value, and commit to? Do we mean the mechanisms of democratic voting? Do we mean consensus building? Or perhaps we mean something else?

The HoM *Questioning and Problem Posing* is another good example. Creating powerful questions is essential for education, but what kinds of questions are we talking about, and for what purpose? Do we mean questions that students should ask when reading to ascertain the credibility and reliability of sources? Or do we mean the development of questions to collect data to inform the creation of hypotheses and further research questions?

Another consideration in curriculum design and HoM is that dispositions should be interdisciplinary and enriched over time. Therefore, what should *Questioning and Problem Solving* look like in mathematics as opposed to in English Language Arts? Or at the end of Grade 2 as opposed to at the end of Grade 12? These points illustrate the richness and complexity of the HoM, and the need to be more focused and intentional when documenting our curriculum.

Within the templates shown in Tables 9.1 and 9.2, one can see that the HoM *Managing Impulsivity* and *Responding with Wonderment and Awe* have been selected as the cognitive dispositions which are deemed necessary for success in this unit. The reader will also notice that not only are the overarching HoM stated, but these have also been articulated in a way that makes it explicit what these HoM actually "look like" in the context of this unit. This has been achieved through the use of the "Five Dimensions of Growth" (Anderson et al., 2008) of Meaning, Capacity, Awareness, Value, and Commitment:

- *Meaning:* A greater ability to articulate more sophisticated definitions and acquire more concepts associated with the HOM. An increased knowledge of an ever-greater range of examples and analogies. The developing prowess to connect HoM to their own experiences and recognize the performance of the HoM in others.
- *Capacity:* Developing strategies and tools used to employ the HoM in increasingly skillful and more complex ways. The capability to employ the HoM with increasing sophistication and accuracy in sequence and concert with other dispositions.
- *Alertness:* Being alert to contextual cues that call for the application of HoM while becoming more self-directed and able to recognize new, novel, and complex situations. Using internal criteria to engage HoM to guide decision making, rather than relying on prompts and support from others. Enlarging the use of the HoM to an ever-increasing range and variety of situations and contexts.
- *Value:* Understanding that there are benefits to engaging HoM and appreciating consequences for not doing so. To truly value the HoM is

to recognise their importance, their benefits, and to prize them over other thinking behaviours.

- *Commitment:* Becoming more self-initiating and self-directed in the executive functions of monitoring and evaluating own performance of the disposition. Becoming more inclined towards and effective in self-managing, self-monitoring and self-modifying the HoM. Autonomously setting realistic, achievable and measurable goals and developing more sophisticated, quantitative and qualitative, and descriptive self-evaluation strategies.

CULMINATING ASSESSMENT

At this point, it is important to look at the culminating assessment for this unit, which is a Performance Task titled "Letter to an Atheist." Students are given the following task to achieve this assessment:

> You will research a religious thinker of your choice, responding to their views on religion, explaining views of religion held by others, and your own personal views. You will also mention examples of religious conflicts and explain how we can handle these conflicts. You will either try to change this person's opinion about religion, or strengthen their opinions by agreeing with them.

This assessment task was designed using the GRASPS template (Goal, Role, Audience, Situation, Product, Specifications; Wiggins & McTighe, 2011):

- *Goal:* Your goal is to provide a balanced and evidence-informed analysis of religion and religious conflict in the modern world. You will then share your views with a religious thinker of your choice via Facebook, Twitter, email, or another method. You will either try to change this person's opinion about religion, or strengthen their opinions by agreeing with them.
- *Role:* You are a concerned citizen of the world who focuses on religion and religious conflicts.
- *Audience:* Your audience is a religious thinker of your choice. This person could be a controversial figure, such as the leader of a radical religious group (Taliban, ISIS, Westboro Baptist Church), or a more mainstream figure, such as a podcaster or religious theologian (Sam Harris, William Lane Craig).
- *Situation:* There is a wide range of opinions on religion. Some believe that their religion is the only way to live a moral life and should be followed by everyone under threat of violence. Some think the world

would be a better place if religion did not exist at all, and that all religions should be illegal. By doing research, you can find people with these extreme views and everything in between.

The performance task is evaluated by the following criteria in the analytic rubric:

- *Identification and analysis of multiple viewpoints on religion:* (Exceeds) Student provides a detailed description of at least two different perspectives on religion with an in-depth explanation of why people hold those views. Student provides a thoughtful analysis of the accuracy of their own views on religion.
- *Conflict Identification, explanation, and Resolution:* (Exceeds) Letter describes in detail several religious conflicts and explains the origins of those conflicts. Thoughtful and in-depth discussion of effective ways to handle these conflicts are discussed. Student includes a detailed look at how the wonderment and/or shock of other religious beliefs and traditions might decrease or increase conflict and misunderstanding.
- *Evidence:* (Exceeds) All claims are supported by evidence and clearly connected to the argument; a wide range of evidence is used, including historic and modern examples. Several primary source quotations are included.

GOALS OF THE UNIT

The unit has three *Transfer Goals.* These have been designed using the concept of Long-term Transfer Goals (LTTGs; Wiggins & McTighe, 2012). The LTTGs should be written to make it absolutely clear to stakeholders how they apply to the particular context of the unit. In this way, a school can develop its own unique set of "Transfer Standards," which not only will guide both students and teachers as to what the overarching learning goals are for students at graduation but will also articulate what those goals look like incrementally across subjects and units, and also through grade levels. The HoM have been integrated into the transfer goals for this unit as follows:

UTG1: Critically appraise primary and secondary sources about religion, including religious texts, for validity and reliability to aid decision making and potential modification of personal worldview.
UTG2: Make informed decisions about religions, and the followers of religions, after analyzing situations from multiple perspectives.

UTG3: Effectively handle religious conflicts and misunderstandings using empathy.

Now that we are clear what the ultimate goals of the unit are, and what evidence is required from students to demonstrate attainment of these objectives, it is easy to see how the HoM *Managing Impulsivity* is useful and vital for students to employ to succeed in the performance assessment. Let's look at the first criteria in the analytic rubric of the *Performance Task*.

Criteria: Identification and Analysis of Multiple Viewpoints on Religion

- UTG: Make informed decisions about religions, and the followers of religions, after analyzing situations from multiple perspectives.
- EQ: Is religion a force for good in the world?
- HoM: Managing Impulsivity

The first point here is the importance of the congruence between the essential question, the HoM and the UTG. If these are all perfectly aligned, then not only can the learner mentally "string-together" all aspects of learning within the unit, but it also becomes much easier for the teacher to design rich learning experiences which cover all the aspects of the desired results as articulated in Stage 1.

The HoM *Managing Impulsivity* has been selected as there is little doubt that it is easy to jump to conclusions about religions and the followers of religions based on several factors such as stereotypes, portrayal by the media, ignorance of history and culture, and the often-metaphorical nature of religious texts amongst others. Going further, it is of vital importance that given the innumerable ways in which one can "manage their impulsivity," it is necessary to put this into context via the lens of the *Five Dimensions of Growth*, the topical content of the unit and the developmental appropriacy of the grade level (or cluster). For this goal, the following three dimensions were featured:

- *Meaning:* Know that employing *Managing Impulsivity* strategies can often lead to hidden and deeper meaning making than jumping to quick conclusions on a topic or viewpoint.
- *Capacity:* Skilled at avoiding hasty judgment on complex issues and viewpoints by employing close reading and listening strategies.
- *Commitment:* Set specific goals to improve listening and reading strategies to avoid jumping to hasty conclusions and judgements on complex topics.

In this way, it crystal clear to both educators and learners alike which cognitive dispositions are necessary for success, rich and engaging learning activities. The following sections discuss considerations for the development of these activities and how they can designed for learners to practice dispositions (HoM), gain feedback on them, self-assess, and set goals for improvement.

DESIGNING LEARNING ACTIVITIES

One of the most important keys to first-class curriculum design is complete alignment among the identified desired results, the evidence collected through rigorous and diverse assessments, and the rich learning activities. This alignment facilitates learning, practice and high-quality and timely feedback (McTighe, 2014). Therefore, just as with more 'traditional' goals, such as the acquisition of knowledge, the attainment of skills, and the development of understanding, it is key that the learner is given ample exposure to learning experiences that allow the practice of the HoM throughout the duration of the unit of study.

The UbD template for a Grade 8 unit on religion determines that for the student to successfully attain the Transfer Goal "Make informed decisions about religions, and the followers of religions, after analyzing situations from multiple perspectives," the *Dimensions of Growth* Meaning, Capacity, and Commitment are all vital for success. Before attempting any Performance Task, the learner needs the opportunity to practice relevant cognitive dispositions, receive feedback, and self-assess and set goals for improvement.

The following learning tasks illustrate how students are given this opportunity. They are tasked with reading the short story *The Last Spin* by Evan Hunter and to identify which HoM is both employed and not employed by the two main characters, and thus has an impact on the plot. The story is based around two gang members who are forced to settle a dispute by playing a game of "Russian roulette." The boys talk as they are playing the game and realize that they have much in common. They start to like each other more and more, and even make some plans together before one of the boys finally loses the game.

The purpose of this activity is for the students to gain an understanding of what the HoM means in the context of not jumping to hasty conclusions about someone (or an idea) before delving in deeper. In addition, if the boys had managed their impulsivity rather than unnecessarily continuing with the game, then a life could have been saved and perhaps a friendship started.

Religion: Managing Impulsivity Activity (Meaning)

Perhaps the best way to illustrate how effective these activities can be is to take a look at how a grade 8 student responded to questions about this disposition. The student is from a school accredited as an *International Habits of Mind Community of Excellence.*

Learning Activity (Meaning)

Directions: After reading the short story *The Last Spin,* answer the following questions:

Questions

1. What habit of mind is most shown being used or failing to be used throughout the story? How do you know?

   Student response: The habit of mind that is most shown failing to be used is Managing Impulsivity because in this story, we can see that the two boys are doing something dangerous without thinking carefully about this Russian roulette because the game will make people lose their lives. So, Dave and Tigo didn't use the HoM Managing Impulsivity carefully.

2. What are two ways the guys failed to use this HoM throughout the story?

   Student response: The two ways the guys failed to use this HoM throughout the story are: The two rival gangs are having disagreements, and the representative to play the game. They fail to use the HoM because there are so many more ways to resolve the conflict, instead they choose this dangerous game. When the two start to bond together talking about their lives together, they didn't stop the game to avoid being harmed, instead they continued making Dave die.

3. What are two ways the guys succeeded at using the HoM throughout the story?

   Student response: The two ways the guys succeeded at using the HoM throughout the story are: When playing the game, during each round, both of them try to talk about something together, so the person playing the round will not be too nervous. When the gangs want them to play the game together, they are very nervous because this game will cause someone to die. However, they are tough and play the game with bravery.

Having looked at the student's work, it is clear that the student has understood that the HoM *Managing Impulsivity* is a key tenet of the plot, and that in the context of the story, *Managing Impulsivity* was both employed and neglected. Feedback from the teacher could involve pointing out how the two boys' feelings changed about one another as they spoke, realizing that they had more in common than they had previously thought. In this way, students can make meaning of the HoM in ways they had perhaps not previously thought about, leading them to new ways of thinking as they journey through the rest of the unit.

The student responses were analyzed using the rubric provided in the previous section. The analysis revealed that the student excelled in these criteria for the following reasons:

- The student is able to identify the correct HoM and give an in-detail explanation as to why they think that way.
- The student is able to explain two ways the guys in the story use the HoM and two ways they fail to use the HoM.
- These explanations are relevant, fit well with the HoM, and are detailed.

Religion: Managing Impulsivity Activity (Capacity)

In the following example, the student is tasked with reading a religious passage (in this case from the Old Testament of the Bible) multiple times, and to employ metacognition (fundamentally the 'precursor' to all of the other HoM) to determine whether she has been too hasty in reaching a conclusion about the text, and therefore the religion itself.

As the student reads the text for a second and then a third time, the student is asked to apply the HoM and to delay reaching a hasty judgment, and to consider whether there may be more metaphorical meanings to the text. Once again, a response from an actual student (different from the previous task), is provided as an example.

Learning Activity (Capacity)

Directions: After reading this Bible verse about revenge, answer the questions:

> *"Elisha went up to the city. As he was walking along the road, some boys came out of the town and made fun of him. 'Get out of here, bald man!' they said. 'Get out of here, bald man!' He turned around, looked at them, and called down a*

curse on them in the name of the Lord. Then two bears came out of the woods and killed forty-two of the boys."

2 Kings 2:23–25

1. After reading the verse one time, do you think the god in this religion is cruel?

    Student response: After reading the verse one time, I think the god in this religion is cruel and not cruel at the same time. Because I think that the forty-two of the boys deserved it because they were humiliating Elisha and making fun of him.

2. After reading the verse for a second time, do you think the verse could mean something else? Or is it literal? Why do you think this way?

    Student response: After reading the verse for a second time, I think the verse could mean something else, like not being literal killing the 42 boys because of 2 bears coming from a demand of God that Elisha had told him. I think that it means that in this religion, people shouldn't criticize other people and respect them at all costs.

3. After reading the verse for a third time, what do you think we can learn about this religion from the verse?

    Student response: After reading the verse for a third time, I think we can learn that this religion shows that people should respect each other and not call them out and being disrespectful to them

A review of the student's work clearly shows how her views evolve as the text is read for the second and third time, and how the student actively employs *metacognition* whilst applying *managing impulsivity* as her thinking changes throughout the process. It is precisely this level of self-awareness that is the goal of incorporating thinking dispositions as explicit goals within the curriculum. The analytic framework showed that this student too exceeded the criteria in the analytic framework presented in the previous section:

- The student is able to explain in detail their initial impulsive reaction to the verse and their justification for this reaction.
- She skillfully use strategies to read between the lines and make inferences from the text to explain if their impulsive reaction is correct or incorrect.
- After managing impulsivity, student explains in detail what we can learn about this religion from this verse

Religion: Managing Impulsivity Assignment (Commitment)

Now that students have been given the opportunity make *meaning* of the HoM in this context, and to practice their *capacity* to apply the HoM, they are given the opportunity to display commitment. Once again, a performance task is given with a sample of a student's work.

Learning Activity (Commitment)

Directions: Answer the questions about your use of the HoM "Managing Impulsivity."

Questions:

1. What score would you give yourself for managing impulsivity (1, 2, 3, or 4)? Why would you give yourself that score?

    Student response: For Managing Impulsivity, I would give myself a score of 2 out of 4. The reason as to why I gave myself a 2 is because while doing the debate on the topic of "Religion is a force for good and positive change in the world," I was able to take my time in going over my statements and the debate prompts as well as taking my time to listen to the opposing team's statements and refuting back. While doing the debate, I would say that I was able to manage my impulsivity and went over everything in my head instead of just rushing through it without thinking.

2. What are three ways that you will be better at using this HoM in the future?

    Student response: Three ways I could do better at using this HoM in the future is one, learning to take my time and going over all my thoughts and ideas, making sure that I'm prepared and that I have everything planned out. Two, if it involves another debate, then I would take my time in listening to the other team's statements and finding ways to rebut back. Lastly, learning to manage my impulsivity and think before I act so that I will get the results I want, which in turn, will help me with applying this HoM better in the future.

3. How will you know when you are better at using the HoM?

    Student response: When I get better at using the HoM, I would be able to know because I would find myself taking more time in doing something, whether it's an activity, lesson or a debate just like this one. I would also learn to take my time and manage my impulsivity so that

I can get the desired outcome, because I took my time in doing and I was able to think before I act. I would see myself taking my time doing something and not rushing, because I'm thinking about what I wanna say and do before actually saying or doing it.

In this case, while the student has done a fair job in self-assessing and goal setting, high-quality feedback would involve asking the student to consider more how well she has applied the HoM to the task of re-evaluating the meaning of complex texts, as opposed to more generally how she has applied it to preparation tasks. Once again, the analytic rubric was used to show the student excelled at meeting the criteria:

- The student has truthfully and correctly scored themself for this HoM with an in-detail explanation.
- The student has written three detailed and relevant strategies so that they will be better at the HoM in the future.
- The student has written how they will know they have used the HOM better with deep explanation.

The example given above is just one example of how a unit can be developed using UbD to incorporate HoM into the curriculum. A few points of clarification should be made here:

- Simply because we are articulating, per unit, the HoM and dimensions which are most applicable for success in the performance assessment, by no means does this mean that we wish to restrict students' thinking to these specific traits. Rather the opposite is true; of course, it is desirable for our students to employ all of the HoM all of the time (or rather develop the alertness as to which ones are desirable and applicable in any given context).
- Likewise, we should not limit student skills when identifying Performance Tasks. For example, in English Language Arts, we happen to be focusing on paragraph organization in a unit, this does not mean that we do not wish our students to use correct spelling, grammar and mechanics in their writing. It is simply a matter of focus, making our planning and instruction intentional and therefore more effective.

MAPPING THE HOM

The aforementioned considerations can be addressed when all the units are created and the HoM are mapped. A guaranteed, viable curriculum from

K-12 needs both horizontal and vertical alignment for desired results. This is to ensure that what we value most in education is adequately covered across all subjects, to eliminate redundancies, and to ensure that key goals 'spiral' through the curriculum at incrementally more sophisticated levels of complexity.

The good news is that work has already begun in this domain. This can be achieved by looking at each unit of study on an individual basis, determining the HoM and the dimensions most applicable to the unit, and then performing a mapping exercise to determine gaps, commonalities and redundancies in order to map out a progression of the HoM across all five dimensions of growth, across all subject areas, and through all grade clusters. The following section explains how developing Competency Standards can help in the mapping process.

DEVELOPING COMPETENCY STANDARDS FOR HOM

The *Five Dimensions of Growth* can be used to develop Competency Standards for the HoM. Following is an example that was created for the HoM *Questioning and Problem Posing* within Grade 12.

- *Meaning:* Students will know that a form of questioning involves the formulation of specific research questions to collect qualitative and quantitative data.
- *Capacity:* Students will be able to ask probing questions to gain qualitative and quantitative data to answer scientific questions.
- *Alertness:* Students will be aware of contexts where it would be beneficial to collect qualitative and quantitative data to answer questions and solve problems.
- *Value:* Students will understand that sophisticated questioning techniques are essential to enable data gathering to support arguments and claims, answer questions, and formulate hypotheses.
- *Commitment:* Students will be able to set SMART goals for improving questioning techniques for research in university and beyond.

These standards can be used to help to map and organize how HoM are addressed in the curriculum. When developing these standards, it is important to consider the following:

- The descriptors for the Competency Standards need to be specific enough to focus planning and instruction on the key 'variant' of the HoM which is needed for success in the unit.

- On the other hand, the descriptors need to be general enough to transcend units within the school level for that subject, and in the best case, transcend multiple subjects to avoid creating a "leviathan" set of competency standards.
- Continual mapping work needs to be undertaken as the work progresses to ensure that competencies are combined where applicable, redundancies are avoided, and that the 'spiraling' up through the school levels is incremental, logical and achievable.
- Before articulating the "commitment" descriptors, it is important to know, or at least have in mind the next incremental level of meaning and capacity for that particular HoM, and within that "domain" of competency (although this can be modified as we go through the process over time).

As additional units are included in the project, these descriptions can be altered and combined to transcend as many units and subjects as possible, therefore creating a streamlined set of HoM Competency Standards that are not too unwieldy and yet are comprehensive enough to "arm" students with a powerful set of cognitive abilities to take them into university and beyond.

By no means is the argument being made that these HoM Competency Standards will encompass every single variation of thinking disposition in every imaginable context. Indeed, the framework is so rich, deep, and powerful that there are almost an infinite number of variations of each. However, what this initiative does achieve is to guarantee that a broad set of variations is addressed in a multitude of contexts, rather than leaving it to chance which our students might discover without intentional planning and guidance.

SUMMARY

Revisiting the guiding questions that this chapter sought to answer, this chapter makes the case that if we are aiming at incorporating the HoM in our curricula, then it is not enough to simply have the intention to do so, or a vague idea that they should be included in instruction. Rather that it is necessary to be mindful, thoughtful, and intentional about how we approach this goal.

This can be achieved by thoughtfully selecting a focused number of HoM which are most applicable to a unit of study, to articulate specifically what the required thinking looks like in that subject and at that grade level across the five dimensions of growth, and then to design learning activities and assessments which focus instruction and give students the opportunities to practice and gain feedback.

It would be remiss of us not to acknowledge the richness and complexity of the HoM. *Thinking and Communicating with Clarity and Precision* looks very different in a grade 2 visual arts class than it does in a grade 11 physical science course. It is paramount that we intentionally think about the nuances of each HoM in the context of each unit before planning our activities and assessments.

While the examples given from this chapter are from the middle school, the HoM are equally as applicable and important at all school levels. Continuing with the example of *Managing Impulsivity,* within a kindergarten unit this might be as simple as knowing that this involves thinking before acting (meaning), developing the skill of controlling emotions (capacity), and under-standing that *Managing Impulsivity* can lead to decreasing the need for trial and error, producing more effective outcomes (value).

In this way, once we have determined what forms the HoM take at the earliest developmental stages, we can increasingly plan for more complexity (depth) and variance (breadth) as we vertically plan our curriculum through the school levels. The final "piece of the jigsaw" is to then map out thee "HoM Competencies" across the curriculum, ensuring that gaps and redun-dancies are addressed, and that complexity spirals appropriately vertically right from kindergarten through grade 12.

We need to have clarity that knowing the meaning of an HoM is very dif-ferent from being able to apply it, which is also different from being aware of a context in which it may be useful and so on. If we are intentional in our curriculum design, then we can ensure that a multitude of meanings across all of the HoM, across all of the dimensions of growth, across all subjects, and across all grade levels are addressed, thus giving our students a comprehen-sive and holistic education in the HoM.

NOTE

1. In all examples within this chapter, in the interests of brevity, only the "exceeds" descriptors of analytic rubrics have been included.

REFERENCES

Anderson, J., Costa, A., & Kallick, B. (2008). Habits of mind: A journey of continu-ous growth. *Learning and Leading with Habits of Mind, 16,* 60.

Barendregt, W., Bekker, T., Börjesson, P., Eriksson, E., & Torgersson, O. (2016). *Legitimate participation in the classroom context—Adding learning goals to participatory design.* https://doi.org/10.1145/2930674.2930686

Krajcik, J., McNeill, K. L., & Reiser, B. J. (2008). Learning-goals-driven design model: Developing curriculum materials that align with national standards and incorporate project-based pedagogy. *Science Education, 92*(1), 1–32. https://doi .org/10.1002/sce.20240

McTighe, J. (2014). *McTighe & Associates—Jay McTighe, author & international education consultant.* https://jaymctighe.com/downloads/Long-term-Transfer -Goals.pdf

Muscott, P. (2018). *A study of the relationship between Habits of Mind and performance task achievement in an international school in South East Asia.* London: University of Roehampton.

Partnership for 21st Century Skills, A. (2008). *21st century skills, education & competitiveness.* https://files.eric.ed.gov/fulltext/ED519337.pdf

Rotherham, A. J., & Willingham, D. T. (2010). "21st-century" skills: Not new, but a worthy challenge. *American Educator, 34*(1), 17–20.

Voogt, J., & Roblin, N. P. (2010). 21st century skills. *Discussienota. Zoetermeer: The Netherlands: Kennisnet.* http://opite.pbworks.com/w/file/fetch/61995295/White %20Paper%2021stCS_Final_ENG_def2.pdf

White, C. B. (2007). Smoothing out transitions: How pedagogy influences medical students' achievement of self-regulated learning goals. *Advances in Health Sciences Education,* 279–297.

Wiggins, G., & McTighe, J. (2011). *The understanding by design guide to creating high-quality units.* ASCD.

Wiggins, G. P., & McTighe, J. (2005). *Understanding by design.* ASCD.

Wiggins, G. P., & McTighe, J. (2012). *The understanding by design guide to advanced concepts in creating and reviewing units.* ASCD.

PART III

Teaching and Assessing Habits of Mind

Chapter 10

Leaning on Habits of Mind in Times of Fear and Uncertainty

Nick Bruski

The Institute for the Habits of Mind has a vision, "To create a more thoughtful, cooperative, compassionate generation of people who skillfully work to resolve social, environmental, economic and political problems." Just over two years ago, the Montecito community was faced with disaster as the combination of the Thomas Fire and Debris Flow devastated the community and forced them to build a remote school from scratch without access to their physical building and community.

With a strong foundation in the Habits of Mind, the community learned countless lessons that continue to help usher them through the new challenges our planet is now facing with the COVID-19 pandemic. As we are asked to stay home, socially distance, wear masks and Zoom, there is no better time to embrace the vision of the Institute for the Habits of Mind.

Our world is full of new social, environmental, and political problems for our children, families, schools, and communities to solve. More than ever we need a thoughtful, cooperative and compassionate society to get us through this time. The following is a first-hand account of how the Habits of Mind can support a community during difficult times, followed by a guide to navigating times of fear and uncertainty using the Habits.

THE THOMAS FIRE AND DEBRIS FLOW: A COMMUNITY STRUCK BY DUAL DISASTERS

The Thomas Fire ignited in December of 2017, which at that time was the largest wildfire in California history, and ravaged nearly 300,000 acres of hillsides and homes, leaving a charred and barren landscape. This damage, combined with incredibly intense rainfalls in the early morning hours of January 9, caused a massive debris flow in the village of Montecito in an around Montecito Union School, destroying homes and taking 23 lives as mud, boulders, branches, vehicles, and even whole homes slid down the mountain.

Montecito Union School's physical structures were spared, sitting at a slightly higher elevation between the two creek beds where most of the destruction happened. However, the community they serve was devastated, facing the loss of friends and family, destroyed, damaged and unlivable homes, contaminated drinking water, a closed highway cutting the town off on the southbound end, weeks of evacuations, and the uncertainty of if and when it would be safe to return to their homes and school.

In the midst of the chaos and the ensuing weeks, their work with the Habits of Mind served as a rock-solid foundation through the immediate trauma of the events, as well as the rebuilding and healing that continued to happen months afterward.

Striving for Accuracy and Precision

As the principal of Montecito Union School, when I awoke on the morning of Tuesday, January 9 and turned on the news, I could not believe the images and videos being displayed; unoccupied foundations where homes used to stand, rivers of mud, and families on rooftops waiting to be rescued. By chance, one of our students was at our home with us on a sleepover, and images of his living room knee-deep in mud were repeatedly shown on the news, causing us to quickly turn off the television whenever he entered the room.

In communicating with our administrative team, we struggled to know where to even begin and how we could support our community at this time. We set out to account for all our families by creating a shared Google Doc listing each of our students. We created a system to account for our families and their whereabouts and circumstances. We shared the document with all our staff and asked them to note any information they had regarding our students and families. We scoured social media and sent messages and emails to check in.

Though many were trapped in homes without phones or Internet, we made phone calls and were able to contact neighbors and friends so that the dozens of staff members striving for accuracy and precision could get the best possible information. Though we were so saddened to learn of the passing of recent alumni and members of legacy families, we were able to announce in a short time that all of our current families escaped the loss of life. The fact that all of our families were accounted for was a powerfully small celebration that set the tone for the coming weeks, while also reinforcing how powerful striving for precision and accuracy can be.

Thinking Flexibly

In the days immediately following the event, there were hundreds of questions and unknowns that we could not answer. With bridges and critical infrastructure damaged and destroyed, some were predicting it could be weeks or maybe even months before roads opened and families would be able to return to their homes. We didn't know if the next rain would cause a similar event and how safe we would be. We also knew that our students needed the normalcy and safety of school, but we could not get to our campus. We had to think flexibly!

For the first two days, we wanted to give our parents some breathing room as well as a chance to be together in community and share their stories. We organized two school-wide "playdates" at local parks where parents could drop their children off so that they could accomplish any critical tasks they needed, such as talking with insurance companies, renting a car, or just buying a toothbrush. Our staff brought games and organized activities, and also set up a "necessities drive" where families could grab toiletries, shoes, clothes, books, and anything else we could get our hands on.

Through a generous partnership with Santa Barbara City College (SBCC), we built a school from scratch in a matter of days. With teachers sometimes sharing an empty classroom with two other classes and some classes even being in an event tent, we were able to have "school" at our local community college. We could not have accomplished this without thinking flexibly. Countless hours were spent thinking through logistics such as how to keep 5-year-olds safe on a college campus, how to manage pick-up, drop-off, recess, music, physical education, and art.

How do we feed 400 students? What about our students with critical medications? How could we operate a school without a phone system? What about books? And pencils? And paper? We brought in portajohns and handwashing stations. We received a generous donation of industrial heaters to keep our three classes in the event tent warm. We put up portable fencing to create an impromptu playground.

We organized a huge team of amazing parent volunteers to direct students between locations and assist with walking them to restrooms and across a college campus. All in all, it was an incredible effort of our staff, our parents and community partnerships that allowed us to build a school from the ground up, providing a sense of stability and normalcy for our students and families during an incredibly trying time.

Fortunately, after six days of school at SBCC, we were informed we could return to our campus! Though the water was not safe to use, we were excited to return, and bringing handwashing stations and bottled water was a small price to pay to be back home. However, we had to continue to think flexibly even upon our return, as our town was evacuated many more times when rain was predicted. We partnered with a neighboring (and aptly named) Hope School District, utilizing empty classrooms, boardrooms, and auditoriums at three different school sites for an additional eight days of school throughout the end of the school year.

Clearly, in the broadest sense we had to think incredibly flexibly to make all of this happen, but there were countless examples of individual flexibility along the way. Teachers created and adjusted lessons on the fly when they did not go as originally planned because of the limitations of sharing a classroom. They taught out of "to go" kits, whatever would fit inside one standard banker's box, each time we evacuated. PE teachers created engaging and fun activities in spaces not designed for PE and with little to no equipment.

Families waited patiently in long pick-up lines and learned new routines, trusting us to keep their children safe. Students adapted to new environments, rules and procedures. Many did not have their backpacks, lunches, or any personal items from home. Once we returned to school, others still lived out of hotels or with friends and families when homes were uninhabitable. Thinking flexibly was a hallmark of our community and was clearly demonstrated these past few months.

"Flexibility is. . . . when you leave your house and you don't worry. A time when I was flexible was at a fire and a mudslide." Madeleine, 1st grade

Listening with Understanding and Empathy

Thinking flexibly helped us endure through the short-term and cope with unusual circumstances. Listening with understanding and empathy helped us heal. Imagine being a young child and trying to comprehend a mountain sliding down and washing away your home. Imagine being afraid every time it rains. Imagine living out of hotels in borrowed clothes and shoes. Imagine being a teacher with a room full of kids who have experienced varied levels of trauma and challenges. Our work with empathy helped us understand that our families were going through tumultuous times and needed us to listen and understand as best we could.

When at SBCC, we established a compassion center where students and families could speak with counselors, take a break from class, and begin to process what had happened. Despite multiple teachers sharing classrooms, we knew this space needed priority and students found a safe place to begin healing. We also made it a priority to create and maintain social opportunities for families to be together, telling stories and supporting one another.

On the night of our annual school dance, our school was once again evacuated. We knew our parents and students needed the opportunity to have fun, to socialize and be together. A local hotel donated their ballroom at a moment's notice and a slew of volunteers created a magical night for our families while once again evacuated and uncertain what that night's rain might bring.

Our classroom teachers also knew the importance of listening with understanding and empathy. They began most days with morning circles where students had the opportunity to talk about their experiences, their fears and worries, and their hopes and dreams. They knew to be patient with the students as students often seemed distracted, frayed, and fragile. They offered support in innumerable ways to families and truly went above and beyond.

Responding with Wonderment and Awe

Though some might expect a community that has gone through so much to feel depressed and victimized, we respond with wonderment and awe at how these events have truly brought out the best in people. Our parents, students, staff, and larger community have engaged in thousands of acts of generosity, kindness, and selflessness. Active GoFundMe pages supported some of our most impacted families to find temporary homes and pay for the most basic needs. Dozens of families surprised a first-grade student (who lost her home) on her birthday with more gifts than you could count.

Families carpooled, loaned cars, lent out spare rooms, and did anything and everything they could to support one another. Local organizations donated funds, materials, equipment, locations, and manpower to help our school get back up and running at our various locations. Parents and community members established the Santa Barbara Bucket Brigade, doing the important work of digging out homes and repairing Montecito through their volunteer corps. We hosted a Night of Heroes to honor all who supported us through these past months with over 200 invitees, and countless more unsung heroes who supported us in unseen ways.

We cannot help but respond with wonderment and awe at the good that exists in everyone and showed itself during these most challenging times. Furthermore, by regularly responding with wonderment and awe and celebrating our small victories publicly, we bolstered the spirit of our community and gave strength to one another throughout this ordeal.

Persistence

Throughout this time our staff and community demonstrated a collective vast amount of persistence. Staff worked well beyond scheduled hours and in straining conditions. Though the future of our village and school had many uncertainties, we had no doubt that we would persist and continue to thrive. Those who lost homes and loved ones would need persistence a great deal, as did those of us who are seeking to assist them. Being well-versed in the Habits of Mind gave our community the strength it needed not just to survive but thrive during a challenging time.

THE HABITS IN THE ERA OF COVID-19

Schools are facing challenges like they have never seen before with the global pandemic of COVID-19. Schools have had to navigate distance learning, masking, social distancing, testing, vaccinations, quarantines and more. School personnel are taxed more than they ever have been before, as well as students and families. This incredibly dynamic situation requires fluent use of the Habits of Mind more than ever before. By embracing the Habits of Mind, communities can find the strength to persevere during these trying times.

Thinking Flexibly

Schools are facing countless decisions on a daily basis that they are not used to answering and are often forced to find creative solutions by *thinking flexibly*. This Habit, more than any other, is critical in times of fear and uncertainty. At the beginning of the stay-at-home order, adults were running laps in their backyards for exercise and "zooming" happy hours to connect socially. Children were having drive-by birthday parties, going to school virtually, and trying to figure out how strict their new "homeschool teachers" were going to be.

Two years into the pandemic, communities are fatigued, still wearing masks, and continually dealing with recurring spikes, testing, masking, and quarantining. Schools are asked to be flexible as the "rules" constantly change. One's quarantine can depend on if your COVID positive or not, if you were masked or not, if and when you received a negative test, if the exposure happened at school or outside of school, if you're a staff member or a student, if you are fully vaccinated or not, and even the definition of being fully vaccinated is continuing to change. Clearly, we must remain flexible to continually adapt to these ever-changing protocols.

In addition to being flexible with these changes in formalized and explicit protocols, school staff need to be flexible in the less explicit and more nuanced day-to-day experiences. As schools are short-staffed and impacted by employee absences, specialist classes get cancelled and teachers must adjust their plans with little warning. Extra duties are added to help cover where needed.

Teachers are having to choose whether they should move ahead with the curriculum when a quarter of their class is absent. They are being asked to teach outside, or with masks on, or with doors and windows open, or with air filters making it difficult to hear. The mental load and number of decisions school staff are making on a daily basis is higher than ever and people are taxed.

The Center for Creative Leadership (CCL) describes three types of flexibility that help with adapting to change: cognitive, emotional, and dispositional (CCL, 2022). They describe cognitive flexibility as, "nimble, divergent thinking, an interest in developing new approaches, the ability to see and leverage new connections, and the propensity to work well across the organization."

As school leaders navigate challenging times, they need to carefully consider new approaches and think outside of the box. How can schedules be rearranged to minimize contact and reduce the risk of exposure to a single positive test? If home rooms are held in person, can specialized classes like music and art be done virtually so that a positive teacher does not expose half of the school? Can parent and staff meetings be held via Zoom to limit exposure and allow those in quarantine to continue to be active participants in their child's education?

Schools are finding creative ways to better serve their community through nimble and divergent thinking. Schools are getting certified as medical labs to provide COVID-19 testing to their communities as well as hosting vaccination clinics on site. Teachers quarantined at home are Zooming for instruction, while students are physically present in the classroom with substitute teachers. All this flexible thinking is an example of cognitive flexibility that is critical for schools to succeed in uncertain times.

When a staff is emotionally flexible, they are comfortable with change. Rather than being dismissive of anxiety, negativity, or resistance to change, they acknowledge and normalize these feelings as part of the change process. Leaders and teachers can facilitate this by making note of feelings when they arise. Give staff time to talk about how they are feeling at the start of each staff meeting with leaders joining inl, sending messages that it is OK to feel this way, while continuing to send positive messages about the direction the school is headed.

Teachers can start each day with a mindful circle, asking students to express their feelings and what they need from one another to help their day be successful. Teachers should also send messages that it is normal to have these feelings and great learning is still going to happen. These activities will build emotional flexibility and normalize the change process, strengthening the school community in a time of fear and uncertainty.

Finally, dispositional flexibility is being able to balance optimism with realism (CCL, 2022). Change is not approached as something to be fearful of, but rather an opportunity to grow and adapt. Whether it is a mudslide or a global pandemic, send messages such as, "Yes, this is going to be hard, but we are serving a critical role to our families in crisis." Leaders and teachers must take care not to downplay how challenging a task may be so as not to be seen as inauthentic but remind them that the community is in this together and will benefit by working together and celebrating small victories where they can be found.

Communities that practice the Habits of Mind are used to meeting change and challenges optimistically and realistically and show grace and patience as school communities navigate change, challenges, fear, and uncertainty. Thinking Flexibly is a potent tool when things get hard. Encourage staff and families to be explicit in naming these opportunities for children and families to practice being flexible. The framework of the Habits of Mind will bring familiarity to unknown times by providing specific tools for children to lean on that they are already familiar with.

When stiudents are frustrated and cannot play with their friends, ask them to think flexibly about other ways to connect and communicate with them. When they are bored at home, ask them to think flexibly about new ways to use old toys. Any time a child is frustrated with an effect this pandemic is having on them, ask them to think flexibly about the situation and find alternative solutions. They may roll their eyes at first, but when used consistently they will develop the habit of thinking flexibly and find ways to adapt to the new normal.

Thinking and Communicating with Clarity and Precision

With change and the need to adapt, it is essential for schools to *think and communicate with clarity and precision*. As the pandemic began, there were many questions to answer. Is remote learning required? Will there be grades? What do students and teachers do if they need help? Technology has made communicating easier than ever, but it can overwhelm the receiver with too much information.

Our school and staff were inundated with well-intentioned offers for free virtual tours and field trips, online subscriptions, and links to thousands of learning resources. We compiled list after list and shared them with families only to find that this caused more stress! Families were overwhelmed with the choices and did not know where to start. During times of anxiety and fear, less is more.

Teachers and administrators must thoughtfully plan how many emails are being sent and how often. Websites need to be updated and streamlined. As parents balanced working from home, supporting their children's learning, managing a household when toilet paper was nearly impossible to find, and worrying about the health of loved ones, they did not have the time to wade through mountains of resources and emails. Keep your communication clear and precise!

Communicating well has continued to be critical as the pandemic has evolved. As mentioned previously, the "rules" are constantly changing and these need to be communicated clearly and precisely to families and staff. The rules are often so complex that written notification may not be enough. For particularly complicated communications, consider recording a video explanation or hosting an online question and answer session.

Another helpful strategy is to anticipate what possible misconceptions or confusions may exist. For example, school communities must navigate the various regulatory bodies that govern them, including the CDC, State Public Health, County Public Health, OSHA, and local board policies. When parents hear on the news that masks are no longer required, does that still hold true in the school setting? Thinking ahead to possible uncertainties and communicating with clarity and precision will save time and energy. Strong and transparent communication builds trust and brings comfort which is critical in times of fear and uncertainty.

Listening with Understanding and Empathy

In order to develop a thoughtful, cooperative and compassionate community, we must *listen with understanding and empathy*. The pandemic brought "new" to everyone, and communities must slow down and understand how everyone is feeling to analyze how well things are working. How are families finding the workload and ease of navigating the technology? Is the amount of teaching and preparation required of teachers reasonable and sustainable? What is it like to teach when you have your own young ones at home?

We surveyed our families shortly after implementing our remote learning plan and received incredible feedback that helped us adjust our course and serve our students even better. We've also had regular check-ins and surveys of staff to understand and empathize with what we are asking of them. Both groups have helped create even more effective and meaningful learning experiences both while Zooming and returning to in-person learning.

During uncertain times, school communities should create opportunities for listening with understanding and empathy for all stakeholder groups. Surveys can be sent for more formalized data. Community forums or "Coffee with the Principal" experiences provide opportunities for parents to give feedback informally. Mindful circles provide students an avenue to respond to prompts and share emotions. Some of the best listening can simply occur by walking around campus and making time to connect with others. Be visible and present and schedule time to be available, particularly during busy and difficult times.

Numerous guides to effective listening can be found with a quick Google search, and when practicing listening with understanding and empathy, it is important to practice the following:

- Avoid distractions and be fully present
- Do not seek to fix the person's problem, but instead focus on ensuring they feel heard by asking questions and seeking understanding
- Try to maintain an open mind and put yourself into the speaker's shoes
- Paraphrase their thinking ensure understanding ("What I hear you saying is . . .")

Though you may not always change your thinking or be able to fix someone's problem, when someone feels heard they feel valued. This skill is critical in times of fear and uncertainty as it works to bring people closer together and continue to build trust. Is your staff feeling overwhelmed and stretched thin? Show that you are listening and minimize unnecessary meetings and pause new initiatives. Are staff members feeling unsafe? Ask them what is making them feel unsafe and what ideas they have to improve the situation. Collaboration starts with listening and will bring your community closer together.

Responding with Wonderment and Awe

As news cycles and headlines might cause some to feel fear and despair, this is also an important time to practice *responding with wonderment and awe*. In our regular busy lives, it is not surprising that we do not slow down and appreciate the little things as much as we should. How can with respond with wonderment and awe to reframe the pandemic as an *opportunity* (remembering to balance being optimistic with realistic). How can we learn to be even better educators through this new challenge? What joys can we find in our simpler daily lives by connecting even more closely with family and reaching out to friends in new and different ways?

When you wake up each morning, do you talk yourself through a list of what is going to be hard about the day, or do you seek opportunities to respond with wonderment and awe to the simpler things in life? Take time to share the positive stories from news and social media with your children. Celebrate the successes and teamwork you are seeing in your school community. Who are those going out of their way to do extraordinary things in service to others? Respond with wonderment and awe to the good in the world and we will send our children strong messages of hope and kindness.

I encourage teachers and families to lean on the Habits of Mind and explicitly use the language of the Habits with their children during times of fear and anxiety. This language and framework empower children and adults by providing tools to make sense of the unknown. It brings familiarity to the unfamiliar. Our modern world has never seen such a dramatic shift in daily life in such a short amount of time and life continues to change on a daily basis. The Habits of Mind serve as a consistent foundation that allows us to approach these times with confidence and optimism.

SUMMARY

Fluent use of the Habits of Mind and explicitly naming theHabits during times of fear and uncertainty brings an element of the known into the unknown. Communities using the Habits feel empowered to tackle challenges and know they have the necessary tools to persevere. Be thoughtful in times of crisis to slow down and consider how the Habits of Mind can support your efforts and reduce anxiety when challenges present themselves.

REFERENCES

Center for Creative Leadership. (January 7, 2022). *Adapting to change requires these 3 types of Flexibility*. CCL. Retrieved January 8, 2022, from https://www.ccl.org/articles/leading-effectively-articles/adaptability-1-idea-3-facts-5-tips/.

Ramachandran, V. (March 1, 2021). *Four causes for "zoom fatigue" and their solutions*. Stanford News. Retrieved January 4, 2022, from https://news.stanford.edu/2021/02/23/four-causes-zoom-fatigue-solutions/.

Chapter 11

The Agile Learner and Learnership

James Anderson

When futurist Alvin Toffler wrote in *Future Shock*, "Tomorrow's illiterate will not be the man who can't read; he will be the man who has not learned how to learn" he was referencing the accelerating rate of change in the world. This applies to today's students more than ever.

Our rapidly changing world means that we can no longer simply teach our students what we think they need to know and then send them out into the world—if we ever could. This generation will have more to learn over the course of their lifetimes than previous generations. They must be lifelong learners, learning continuously so they can adapt as the world transforms around them.

However, it's not just the rate of change, and amount of learning that comes with it, that is the issue. It's also the nature of that change. Our youth are growing up in a world that is more volatile, uncertain, complex, and ambiguous (VUCA) than it has ever been before. And that means that the world is a more challenging place than it has ever been. Not only will this generation have more problems to solve in their lifetime, but the nature of the problems will become increasingly difficult. This increasing difficulty will require learners to behave in increasingly intelligent ways.

To be prepared for this rapidly changing, increasingly complex world, students must develop a deep appreciation of themselves as learners. They must recognize that learning is not simply about using their existing abilities to learn more. Rather, it's about creating new abilities and becoming better, more skillful learners. They must understand that when they encounter problems beyond their current abilities they can develop new talents, learn to behave more intelligently and, ultimately, succeed at increasingly difficult problems.

What does it mean to behave more intelligently and develop abilities that allow you to succeed at increasingly complex problems? A significant part of learning to behave more intelligently is about developing your Habits of Mind.

Professor Art Costa and Dr. Bena Kallick describe the Habits of Mind as dispositions that are skilfully and mindfully employed by characteristically successful people when confronted with problems, *the solutions to which are not immediately apparent*. In other words, these are the behaviors that learners must engage in to stretch and grow to solve more and more complex problems. The Habits of Mind are the behaviors that ultimately lead to that growth.

However, it's not enough to simply use your Habits of Mind to solve problems. As those problems become increasingly difficult, learners need to develop, improve, and get better at how they engage their Habits of Mind. Moreover, how they go about achieving that improvement becomes critical. The most skilful learners not only develop, but rather cultivate their Habits of Mind, as they develop what I call Learnership.

As Lisa Christensen, Jake Gittleson, and Matt Smith (2020) point out in their article, "The most fundamental skill: Intentional learning and the career advantage" for McKinsey and Company, an increasing body of research is demonstrating that learning itself is a skill, and developing it is a critical driver of career success. Today's students will need to develop Learnership in order to get better at getting better. And the most skilful learner is the 'agile learner.'"

It is the agile learner that is best prepared for the VUCA world this generation faces. An agile learner is the learner that not only understands they are capable of growth, but also understands how to go about achieving that growth. And this prepares them to thrive in an unpredictable future.

Let's dive into the elements of the growth mindset, describe the qualities of the agile learner and discover how, by embracing challenge and cultivating their Habits of Mind, learners can thrive in the type of world described by Toffler as the future.

A GROWTH MINDSET

A growth mindset is a critical foundation to a learner's work with the Habits of Mind and their development as skilful learners.

People with a fixed mindset don't understand the true nature of learning. They believe their abilities are fixed and unchangeable, and that learning is about discovering what those abilities are. When they encounter challenges beyond their current abilities, they'll say things like, "I'm just not very good at thinking flexibly." Or they might attribute success to *having* those abilities.

They might say things like, "I succeeded because I strive for accuracy." For these people, the Habits of Mind become a labeling exercise to describe what some learners can do and other learners can't.

On the other hand, learners with a growth mindset understand that learning is about growth, improvement, development and creating new abilities. When they encounter problems beyond their current abilities, they recognize that they can develop their Habits of Mind to better tackle these problems. They'll say things like, "I'll need to get better at thinking flexibly," or recognize that "I'm currently not very good at managing my impulsivity. I'll need to get better at that."

While the contrast between a fixed mindset and growth mindset is useful for understanding the importance of Dweck's work, the reality is that most people fall along a continuum between fixed and growth. As Dweck writes, "Everyone is actually a mixture of fixed and growth mindsets, and that mixture continually evolves with experience. A pure 'growth' mindset doesn't exist, which we have to acknowledge in order to attain the benefits we seek."

So, the more growth-oriented we become, the more we understand ourselves as learners capable of creating new abilities and developing our Habits of Mind.

A growth mindset leads agile learners to go beyond *using* their Habits of Mind, to *improving* them. They recognize that to succeed at increasingly difficult tasks, they must get *better* at their Habits of Mind. They understand that "what got me here, won't get me there." So agile learners seek to deliberately improve how they engage in the Habits of Mind. They understand that they can make previously unattainable challenges achievable by developing their Habits of Mind.

But believing that you can develop your talents and abilities is different from actually achieving that development. This highlights one of the biggest misunderstandings about Dweck's work: a growth mindset is not growth. It tells us, *I can grow*, but it doesn't tell us how to achieve that growth. An agile learner does more than believe in their ability to grow; they understand *how* to *achieve* that growth.

CHALLENGE AND THE LEARNING ZONE

Without challenge, there can be no growth. Agile learners understand that it is only by challenging themselves to go beyond their current best, that they can hope to improve and successfully confront increasingly challenging problems.

Many of the so-called "challenges" that students take on are not challenging at all. Instead, they are well within their current abilities, with solutions

that are immediately apparent to them. Because they are relatively uncompli-
cated, these "challenges" feel more like *tasks*—chores within their comfort
zone and easily completed by applying their current Habits of Mind. While
these challenges might be new to the students, and take time and energy to
complete, they are simply "easy things they haven't done yet" and don't
result in growth.

These tasks provide learners with the short-term satisfaction of completion
but deny them the long-term benefit of growth that only comes from stepping
outside the comfort zone. Spending time in their comfort zone gives them
an illusion of growth as they tick off task after task. It keeps them busy and
getting things done. But the agile learner understands that getting busy isn't
as good as getting better!

Agile learners know that stepping outside their comfort zone means
attempting something just beyond their current abilities. This pushes them
into what we refer to as the "learning zone" (also referred to as the Zone of
Proximal Development).

The learning zone involves stretch, challenge, and effort. It comes with the
uncertainty of not immediately knowing the solution, and the risk of failure.
But agile learners get comfortable with the discomfort of their learning zone.
They see challenge as a desirable difficulty because it gives them the opportunity to grow. They recognize that effort is the currency of growth and are
prepared to invest effort to help them along the way.

In the words of expert Anders Ericsson, co-author of *Peak: Secrets from
the New Science of Expertise*, "This is a fundamental truth about any sort
of practice: If you never push yourself beyond your comfort zone, you will
never *improve*." Agile learners not only seek out these types of challenges
but embrace them for the opportunity they provide for cultivating their
Habits of Mind.

Agile learners understand that growth and improvement come from
stretching beyond their current best to find challenges that demand more of
them than in the past. These are the types of challenges that demand more
well-developed Habits of Mind and eventually make a learner's best, better.

Agile learners also understand that by challenging themselves, they "raise
the bar." They not only succeed at that particular challenge, but because their
newly developed Habits of Mind are (largely) transferable, they are better
prepared for challenges they haven't encountered yet. This makes challenges
that would have previously been impossible, possible. This has the effect of
future proofing learners, and as we'll see below, making them anti fragile, one
of the long-term benefits of growth.

DEVELOPING HABITS OF MIND

As we discussed, Habits of Mind are the behaviours learners must engage in when they step beyond their current best, outside of their comfort zone and into their learning zone. The Habits of Mind are the behaviors that ultimately lead to growth and allow us to find solutions to problems.

But they're not one dimensional. Learners don't simply *use* them when confronting problems. They must learn to use them *well* and apply them in increasingly sophisticated and mature ways. Anyone who wishes to succeed at increasingly difficult tasks, must constantly be developing their Habits of Mind to match.

Everyone experiences challenges that are beyond their current abilities as being difficult, demanding or just plain hard! But these terms are all *relative* terms. There is nothing inherently "hard" about a problem. It's only hard compared to the learner's current abilities.

Consider a problem you found hard when you were 10 years old. Chances are you'd find the same problem—and even similar problems you've never encountered—easy today. That's because you've developed your Habits of Mind since then. You're literally smarter today than you were when you were 10. A challenge that was in your learning zone is now in your comfort zone. This what developing your Habits of Mind does. It makes hard things easy!

Albert Einstein is widely misquoted as saying, "We can't solve problems by using the same kind of thinking we used when we created them." While this might not come from the man in these exact words, the sentiment holds. Agile learners understand this. They know that to succeed at increasingly difficult tasks, they must learn to become better thinkers. By developing their Habits of Mind, they learn how to behave more intelligently, succeed at more challenging tasks, and constantly push at the edges of their learning zone.

To improve their Habits of Mind learners must first understand what that improvement looks like. Simply saying, "I need to get better at thinking flexibly" doesn't tell you what you need to do to improve. And that's where the "dimensions of growth" come in.

5 Dimensions of Growth

In *Learning and Leading with Habits of Mind*, Costa and Kallick describe five ways to get better at the Habits of Mind. These dimensions of growth are:

1. *Meaning:* The *what* of the Habits of Mind. As you develop a Habit of Mind, you come to understand its meaning in more depth. You can draw on richer examples and define it with added depth and precision.

2. *Capacity:* The *how* of the Habits of Mind. Each Habit of Mind encompasses a range of specific skills, tools, and strategies. Improvement is reflected in a growing repertoire of these, as well as an increased sophistication in how you use them.
3. *Alertness:* The *when* of the Habits of Mind. Each challenge demands the application of a specific subset of the Habits of Mind. This dimension is about identifying which Habits of Mind are appropriate to specific challenges and becoming more attuned to the signals, cues, and indicators that alert you to an opportunity to call upon those Habits.
4. *Value:* The *why* of the Habits of Mind. As you mature in a Habit of Mind, you'll come to recognize more deeply the benefits that arise. Consequently, you're more likely to choose to engage in that Habit over other less productive patterns of behavior.
5. *Commitment:* The *how well* of the Habits of Mind. This dimension speaks to your ability to self-assess, self-direct, and self-modify how you are engaging in the Habits of Mind. As you develop in the Habits you become increasingly accurate and qualitative in your assessment, as well as increasingly self-directed in driving your development.

Taken together these dimensions of growth give you the focus you need to develop your Habits of Mind. Agile learners are very attuned to getting better at the Habits of Mind and using these dimensions of growth to guide their development.

LEARNERSHIP: THE SKILL OF LEARNING

The distinguishing feature of an agile learner is not simply that they take on challenges, or that they develop their Habits of Mind. Rather it's about how they go about doing these things. The agile learner is a very skilful learner, one who engages in learning in the most efficient and effective ways. And they are the only truly lifelong learners.

In *The Learning Landscape: How to Increase Learner Agency and Become a Lifelong Learner,* I describe six different types of learners (see Figure 11.1). These learners vary in five key elements of learning:

1. How they build their relationship with challenges
2. How they go about developing their Habits of Mind
3. How they respond to and acquire information for learning from mistakes
4. How they gather and learn from feedback
5. How they use their time and energy

LEARNERSHIP: THE SKILL OF LEARNING
James Anderson

	CHALLENGE	HABITS OF MIND	MISTAKES	FEEDBACK	TIME & ENERGY
AGILE LEARNER	EMBRACES	CULTIVATES	DESIGNS	TAILORS	GROWING
INDEPENDENT LEARNER	TARGETS	DEVELOPS	USES	REQUESTS	STRIVING
DIRECTED LEARNER	ATTEMPTS	EXTENDS	CORRECTS	RESPONDS	PRODUCING
PERFORMANCE LEARNER	LIMITS	APPLIES	AVOIDS	SELECTS	PERFORMING
BEGINNER LEARNER	REDUCES	DESCRIBES	RECOGNISES	ACKNOWLEDGES	DOING
NON-LEARNER	AVOIDS	IGNORANT	IGNORES	DISREGARDS	WASTES

www.jamesanderson.com.au/learnership

Figure 11.1. The Learnership Matrix. *Author created and copyrighted.*

By looking at the way learners vary in their approach to these elements, we can define six different types of learners, from the least skilled non-learner to the highly skillful agile learner.

Different learners respond to challenge and the development of their Habits of Mind in different ways. Non-learners, beginning learners, and performance learners are all "below the bar" learners. These learners remain in their comfort or performance zones, avoiding the discomfort and uncertainty of their learning zone. Consequently, there is little, if any, true growth.

Directed learners rely on a teacher to grow. They will attempt challenges and extend their Habits of Mind at the direction of a teacher or a parent. While the directed learner does grow, their growth is driven by the adult who is controlling the learning process. In the absence of a teacher to guide this learning, growth stops.

Independent learners set their own goals and develop their Habits of Mind as necessary to achieve each goal. For the independent learner, their goal is their priority and developing their Habits of Mind are a means to achieving their goal. However, in the absence of a goal, growth may stop.

Agile learners take the Habits of Mind to the next level. They see Habits of Mind as a long-term asset, and the long-term benefit of growth as the most valuable outcome of learning. Rather than using Habits of Mind as a means for achieving their goal, the agile learner sees the challenge as a means for developing their Habits of Mind—a potentially once in a lifetime opportunity for growth.

Agile learners recognize the relationship between challenge and specific Habits of Mind. They understand that different challenges give them opportunities to develop specific Habits of Mind. They are very aware of where their relative strengths and weaknesses in the Habits of Mind lie. And they deliberately select challenges for the opportunities they provide for developing areas they see as needful. In this way they don't merely develop, but instead *cultivate* their Habits of Mind.

In this way, agile learners reflect the spirit of late U.S. President John F. Kennedy when he famously announced the Apollo spaceflight program: "We choose to . . . do these . . . things, not because they are easy, but *because they are hard.*"

This is why agile learners are the only true lifelong learners. Directed learners grow only in the presence of the teacher. Independent learners grow only in the presence of their goals. But the world will always, and increasingly, provide challenges to be embraced. While the agile learner continues to seek challenges that stretch them in new ways, they will continue to be a source of continuous growth.

FUTURE PROOFING AND BECOMING ANTI-FRAGILE

In education we know that we are preparing students for "jobs that have not yet been created, for technologies that have not yet been invented, to solve problems that have not yet been anticipated." Agile learners know that because of the VUCA nature of the future, it is unavoidable that they going to be presented with challenges that they are currently unprepared for.

In his book, *Antifragile*, author Nassim Nicholas Taleb says, "We cannot predict the future, but we can prepare for it." Taleb's work on things that are "anti-fragile" is also highly relevant to our discussion. The concept of something being anti-fragile is not one that most people intuitively understand.

When considering the opposite of fragile (*anti*-fragile), many people think of "robust" or "resilient." But these are not the opposite of fragile. To be robust or resilient simply means an object can withstand disruptions without breaking or returning to its original state.

The opposite of fragile—something that is "anti-fragile"—actually *benefits* from disruption, or in this case, a challenge. It grows stronger and better adapted *because of a challenge*.

For example, think of the way many plants recover from a good prune. These plants could be described as anti-fragile because when they grow back, they don't return to their original state, but are stronger and lusher. They improve and benefit from the disruption of a decent prune, more so than they would from being left alone.

Anti-fragile systems can grow and adapt, while resilient systems simply weather the change, until the change becomes too extreme, and they break.

Taleb cites many examples in the natural world that are anti-fragile, including evolution and the human immune system.

Agile learners are anti-fragile. They respond to challenge and adversity with growth that adapts them to the new environment. They embrace challenges as potentially once-in-a-lifetime learning opportunities and leverage them to develop their Habits of Mind. Consequently, the agile learner has greater agency in the world and can positively influence the world around them and succeed at increasingly difficult problems. In a VUCA world, the resilient might survive, but the anti-fragile will thrive!

SUMMARY

As educators it is our role to prepare students for the future. In order to succeed, our students must first understand themselves as learners, so we need to move them along the mindset continuum and help them develop an increasingly growth-oriented mindset. Then we must help them develop as agile learners, ones that embrace challenges and cultivate their Habits of Mind to proactively prepare for a challenging and unpredictable future.

REFERENCES

Anderson, J. (2010). *Succeeding with habits of mind: Developing, infusing and sustaining the habits of mind for a more thoughtful classroom.* Hawker Brownlow Education.

Anderson, J. (2019). *The learning landscape: How to increase learner agency and become a lifelong learner.* Hawker Brownlow Education.

Anderson, J. (2021). *The agile learner: Where growth mindset, habits of mind, and practice unite.* Solution Tree.

Anderson, J. (n.d.). *Future proof your students: The role of learnership and habits of mind.* Accessed at https://www.jamesanderson.com.au/blog/future-proof-your-students-the-role-of-learnership-and-habits-of-mind.

Anderson, J. (n.d.). *Learnership: The skill of learning.* James Anderson. Accessed at www.jamesanderson.com.au/learnership

Christensen, L., Gittleson, J., & Smith, M. (August 7, 2020). The most fundamental skill: Intentional learning and the career advantage. *McKinsey Quarterly.* Accessed at https://www.mckinsey.com/featured-insights/future-of-work/the-most-fundamental-skill-intentional-learning-and-the-career-advantage.

Costa, A., & Kallick, B. (2008). *Learning and leading with habits of mind: 16 essential characteristics for success.* ASCD.

Dweck, C. (January 13, 2016). What having a "growth mindset" actually means. *Harvard Business Review.* Accessed at https://hbr.org/2016/01/what-having-a-growth-mindset-actually-means

Ericsson, A., & Pool, R. (2016). *Peak: Secrets from the new science of expertise.* HarperOne.

Giles, S. (May 9, 2018). How VUCA is Reshaping the Business Environment and What it Means for Innovation. *Forbes.* Accessed at https://www.forbes.com/sites/sunniegiles/2018/05/09/how-vuca-is-reshaping-the-business-environment-and-what-it-means-for-innovation/?sh=76dde4c5eb8d.

History up close: Kennedy podium [Video]. YouTube. Accessed at https://www.youtube.com/watch?v=s4TJJbhKhuo&t=3s.

OECD. (2018). *The future of education and skills—Education 2030.* Accessed at https://www.oecd.org/education/2030/E2030%20Position%20Paper%20(05.04.2018).pdf

Taleb, N. N. (2014). *Antifragile: Things that gain from disorder.* Random House Trade.

Toffler, A. (1999). *Future shock.* Bantam Dell.

Vygotsky, L. S. (1978). *Mind in society: The development of higher psychological processes.* Massachusetts: Harvard University Press. Accessed at http://csieme.us/documents/Example-Annotated-Bib.pdf

Chapter 12

Developing Habits of Mind through Character Education

Erika Elkady and David Bauzá-Capart

"The function of education is to teach one to think intensively and to think critically. Intelligence plus character—that is the goal of true education."

—Martin Luther King, Jr.

WHAT IS THE PURPOSE OF EDUCATION?

For much of the twentieth century as well as the twenty-first a global trend towards academic achievement has resulted in an over-emphasis on the instrumental aspects of teaching. This has in our opinion been to the detriment of what we consider good education as we see a narrowing of the curriculum and a removal of the ethical role of the teacher (Arthur et al., 2017; Campbell, 2008).

We are probably speaking on behalf of many colleagues working in schools globally when we say that we did not join the profession preparing our students for a "life of tests." We did not become teachers worrying about league tables. We did not expect having to follow up on detailed rules and procedures to be "inspection-ready." Most of us became educators because we feel it is a calling. A desire to make a difference in a young person's life. We are teachers because we want our students to do well and truly flourish in life. We want them to be morally good people who understand and feel what is "good" and most importantly also act morally.

However, many of us have become disillusioned with the profession, and contemplated to change careers or if financially possible, retire early. Moreover, and this is equally concerning, many young people have no desire to become teachers as the profession has seemingly lost status and is by many considered to be compensated poorly (Loewus, 2021). The global shortage of teachers has been making headlines for years as schools have been struggling to fill vacancies (Unesco, 2021).

Martin-Kniep and Kallick (2021) summarize the above-described situation as follows: "Teachers are immersed in a world that is now plagued by initiatives, labels, and tasks, where it's easy to lose sight of what is at the heart of teaching and learning." As a result, this world is not only making many teachers feel burned-out, disillusioned, and helpless, it is also harmful to many students who have lost interest and motivation to do well in school.

It may not be a surprise that one of the most watched Ted Talks of all time is by the late Sir Ken Robinson who addressed in 2006 "How schools kill creativity" and what this does to students (Ted, 2006). Although we do not want to solely blame the increase in school dropouts as well the upsurge of mental illnesses in young adolescents to the current instrumental practice in education, we also can't deny that it has been a contributing factor (Gleason, 2017; Robinson, 2015).

Going back to the original question: *What is the purpose of education?* The results of the school's Dubai Student Wellbeing Census pointed out that our students did not rate their wellbeing as what we had expected it to be. The somewhat gloomy reality sank in further when GL's Pupils Attitudes to Self and School (PASS) confirmed a rather similar outcome. We realized that we had to make things better and not only for our students but also for our community. And so, we decided to be the system changers Robinson (2015), Schwartz and Sharpe (2010) encourage schools to be by embarking upon a journey to teach happiness and wellbeing in our school.

However, the question we asked ourselves was, *How do we teach happiness and wellbeing?* We went back to the ancients for advice. Aristotle (2004), in his *The Nicomachean Ethics*, explains that *eudaimonia* [flourishing] is the happiness that is to be found in the living of a life (opposed to *hedonic* happiness which is a more shallow, short-lived pleasure). Aristotle felt that the aim of education was the development and habituation of virtues which would lead to a life well-lived. This active state of *eudaimonia* would be acquired over a lifetime (Aristotle, 2004).

Kristjánsson (2015, p. 25) clarifies this further: "A term such as 'the flourishing child' must thus not be understood as referring to a child who has achieved flourishing but to a child who is successfully on the way to leading a good life." Therefore, actualization of the virtues must be seen as both conducive and constitutive of flourishing. Although we felt that Aristotle had given us purpose, we realized that we needed a road map and compass to guide us on the journey.

After a year of reading, discussions, and learning we decided that neo-Aristotelian Character Education would be our navigation system to help us find our way (back) to what we consider the real purpose of education: helping our students to flourish as human beings (Jubilee Centre, 2017). There were other paths besides character education to choose from: moral education, social-emotional learning, positive education, values education, and habits of mind to name a few. As mentioned above, we chose to introduce character education and did so for several reasons:

1. Character education has been around for some time as it goes back to ancient times. Character education is therefore in our opinion not the latest fad and is here to stay.

2. We believed that all teachers are teachers of character as we are "care-givers, role-models, and mentors; creators of caring and democratic classroom environments; moral discipline practitioners; teachers of values through the curriculum; developers of cooperative learning; the conscience of the craft; ethical reflection; and teachers of conflict resolution" (Lickona, 1997). As every school has its own ethos, its policies and reward systems and ways in which people interact with each other, we had to make what Arthur (2003, p. 118) refers to as the "hidden curriculum" more tangible. What we felt we had to do first was to review our vision, mission and values and make these explicit in all we do, outside but also inside the classroom.

3. We found that character education—as advocated by the Jubilee Centre—to be a natural fit with the IB educational philosophy and as Jumeira Baccalaureate School is an IB Continuum School this made character education a logical choice. We did not want our teachers to see character education as an "add on" to their already busy plates but more as an endorsement underwriting, highlighting and further promoting what we as IB teachers are expected to do; teaching and modeling the IB learner profile traits, the approaches to learning skills, international mindedness, and providing service-learning opportunities which are all virtues and/ or promote virtuous behavior.

    Berkowitz (2021, p. 33) says it best when he states that "good character education is good education." So, we assured our teachers that they were not doubling up on work as developing character qualities (e.g., critical thinking, reflection, autonomy, resourcefulness, and so on) are important assets for all good learners. Character education, therefore, would reinforce and complete our curriculum.

4. Although the main aim of character education is flourishing individuals and society, the happy side-effect of improved student outcomes was seen as a welcome bonus too (Arthur et al., 2017; Berkowitz, 2021; Kristjánsson, 2015; Watts et al., 2021).

Summary: The purpose of education is to help students flourish as human beings and at JBS we have decided to develop the principles of character education to achieve it.

WHAT IS CHARACTER? WHAT IS CHARACTER EDUCATION AND WHY IS IT IMPORTANT?

Character is "a set of personal traits or dispositions that produce specific moral emotions, inform motivation and guide conduct (Jubilee Centre, 2017)." These character traits are also called virtues and as mentioned before Aristotelian inspired virtue ethics make a direct connection from the education and habituation of virtues to human flourishing. In this philosophy, character strengths or virtues enable us to do the right thing at the right time for the right reason (Harrison et al., 2016). The habituation of virtues in young people will therefore not only help them when they leave school, they are also important for them whilst at school.

The Jubilee Centre (2017) categorizes virtues, which most teachers will recognize as learning skills, in four virtue types which are known as the building blocks of character. These virtue types are: *intellectual virtues, moral virtues, civic virtues,* and *performance virtues*. Moreover, there is an overarching intellectual meta-virtue called phronesis or practical wisdom. Practical wisdom or 'good sense' is "the overall quality of knowing what to want and what not to want when the demands of two or more virtues collide, and to integrate such demands into an acceptable course of action (Jubilee Centre, 2017, p. 4)."

Moral Virtues

The prioritization of the moral values as advocated by neo-Aristotelian character educationists is what really resonated with us on our quest to find a navigation system guiding us to a flourishing school. Brooks (2015) explains this well in his book *The Road to Character* when he makes the distinction between résumé virtues and eulogy virtues.

The first type is what our employers may be most interested in. These are the performance and intellectual virtues which help to achieve external success. The eulogy virtues are those which almost all of us would like to hear at our own funeral: "s/he was kind, compassionate, caring, honest and humble." These are the virtues that really define our character.

Since most schools including IB Diploma schools tend to focus on the performance and intellectual virtues (Gleason, 2017), we felt the need to bring the moral virtues to the forefront. Not only because we too often hear about politicians, businesspeople, entertainers, and athletes who make the news due to their character flaws but mainly because all the other virtues need to be guided by moral virtues. As Kristjánsson (2015, p. 6) explains with humor: "What we want to instil in kids is not the grit of the repeat offender," which is exactly why we applaud the perseverance displayed by young Kevin McCallister and not that of Harry and Marv in *the Home Alone* movies (Columbus, 1990).

Performance Virtues

The performing virtues are often considered "skills for life and work" and are more commonly known (and incorrectly labelled) as "soft skills," "non-cognitive skills" and "social emotional skills." The performance-driven view of character has become popular by Paul Tough's book *How Children Succeed* (2012). Positive psychologists such as Carol Dweck (2006) and Angela Duckworth (2016) also advocate that schools should focus on the development of grit and self-control, so students do well academically.

From the above it may be clear that neo-Aristotelian character educationists (Arthur et al., 2016; Kristjánsson, 2015) reject the idea of the promotion of performance virtues *without* the cultivation of moral virtues. Moreover, Kristjánsson (2015, pp. 22–23) warns not to replace "the one-sided focus on league tables and high stakes testing" with "new ways of harnessing grades through 'character.'"

Intellectual Virtues

These virtues are most linked with learning and school. The IB promotes intellectual virtues such as critical thinking, creative problem solving, independent learning, curiosity, and resourcefulness through the approaches to learning skills. The vast majority of the Habits of Mind could be considered as intellectual virtues (see Tables 12.1 to 12.3). Wagner (2008) and Wagner and Dintersmith (2015) see these virtues as most important as they call them 'the survival skills' which are needed in a globalized, innovation era. Costa and Kallick (2008, p. xxiii) are likely in agreement as they consider the HoM a response to "the shift to a digital age that values intellectual capital."

The Civic Virtues

Civic virtues are seen as the active, social expression of the moral virtues such as compassion and courage. The civic virtues are prominent in IB schools as they fall under the compulsory requirement of service learning. Civic virtues do not only help students "to feel good by doing good," but they are also seen as ways to empower students and increase student voice by making a positive impact on a local, national, and international level.

Summary: Character education is the development of positive (morally good) character traits (virtues) which will help students to become practically wise and flourish. Positive character traits are divided into building blocks (intellectual, moral, civic, and performance) and need to become habits.

CHARACTER EDUCATION AND THE HABITS OF MIND

From the above, it may be clear that character education "includes all explicit and implicit educational activities that help young people develop positive personal strengths called virtues" (Jubilee Centre, 2017, p. 2). Therefore, character education is much more than a school subject. Berkowitz (2021, p. 5) calls character education "first a way of being and then a way of doing." What he means is that what we feel in our hearts and what we think in our minds (i.e., our character) affects what we do.

Aristotle said it as follows: "The aim of education is not just to know what virtue is, but to become good" (Jubilee Centre, 2017, p. 1). The ultimate aim of character education is therefore for students to develop good sense; making the right decision in challenging situations which "arises gradually out of the experience of making choices and the growth of ethical insight" (Jubilee Centre, 2017, p. 2). This will allow individuals and society to flourish.

From the above, it may be clear that there are many similarities between character education and the Habits of Mind [HoM]. Both aim "to elevate the curriculum" from the current focus on standards and accountability. Both are approaches to develop virtues or dispositions in students. Like virtues, the HoM "become intuitive, ultimately reaching automaticity" (Costa & Kallick, 2008, p. 53) and in Aristotelian fashion they "are never fully mastered, for continuous learners they are continually practiced, modified, and refined" (Anderson et al., 2008, p. 62).

Virtues and HoM are not only explicitly taught they are also caught as teachers are seen as role models (Costa & Kallick, 2008, p. 55). Finally, they both impact the ethos or culture of the school (Costa & Kallick, 2008, p. xviii). However, there are some differences too. As mentioned before the HoM focus on the intellectual virtues as they are "a set of valued intellectual dispositions" (Costa & Kallick, 2008, p. 42) which are seen as the attributes of successful people which "we should help our students acquire [these attributes] as well" (Costa & Kallick, 2008, p. 1).

The purpose of the HoM is to prepare students for the digital age and to become successful; "not only in school but also in life" (Costa & Kallick, 2008, p. 56). The omission of moral virtues will likely make Kristjánsson reflect on the importance of morality when discussing the meaning of "success" (e.g., Is the corrupt banker successful?). However, we are reassured that when we take the HoM together "they are a force directing us toward increasingly authentic, congruent and ethical behavior. They are the touchstone of integrity and the tools of disciplined choice making" (Costa, 2008, p. 40).

Nevertheless, the explicit emphasis on moral virtues, civic virtues and the mega-virtue of practical wisdom seem to be the main differences between the HoM and neo-Aristotelian character education. Tables 12.1, 12.2, and 12.3 show how the 16 HoM overlap with the building blocks of character and the IB approaches to learning (ATL) skills, whilst also signifying the HoM prioritization of the intellectual virtues.

IMPLEMENTING CHARACTER EDUCATION AT JBS

As mentioned above, the introduction of character education at JBS was a decision made by the school leaders. Our prioritization of character education meant that we first had to get our stakeholders on board so we could collectively revise our vision, mission, and core values and present this to the wider school community. At the time of writing this chapter, there is a new review on its way.

As practical wisdom dictates, we learn from past experiences, built on this and are always moving forward to develop our practice further (Harrison, 2016). Our recruitment strategy has changed and whilst we still focus on attracting teachers who know their subject and know how to teach well, the emphasis is now on hiring teachers who want "to teach children first."

Whilst people are often hired for their qualifications and experience, we are foremost focussing on the character of the applicant. The Jubilee Centre (2015, p. 1) states that "the single most powerful tool a teacher has to impact on a student's character is their own character." We can all relate to this as we remember our favorite teachers for their positive character traits (as well as our least favorite teachers for their character flaws) than what they taught us.

Table 12.1. Similarities between HoM, Building Blocks of Character, IBLP Traits, and ATL Skills

Habits of Mind	Building Blocks of Character	IB Learner Profile Traits	ATL Skill Category, Cluster, and Indicator (IB)
1. Persisting	Performance		Self-Management; IV. Affective • Managing state of mind • Perseverance
2. Managing impulsivity	Performance	Balance	Self-Management; IV. Affective • Managing state of mind Emotional management
3. Listening with understanding and empathy	Performance Moral	Caring, open-minded	Social; II. Collaboration skills • Working effectively with others • Practice empathy • Listen actively to other perspectives and ideas
4. Thinking flexibly	Intellectual	Caring, open-minded, thinker, inquirer	Thinking; VIII. Critical-thinking skills • Analyzing and evaluating issues and ideas Thinking; IX. Creative-thinking skills • Practice flexible thinking
5. Thinking about thinking	Intellectual Moral	Reflective, caring	Self-Management; V. Reflection skills • (Re) considering the process of learning; choosing and using ATL skills
6. Striving for accuracy	Performance Moral	Principled, caring, knowledgeable	Research; VI. Information Literacy • Collect, record, and verify data
7. Questioning and posing problems	Intellectual	Inquirers	Thinking; VIII. Critical-thinking skills • Analyzing and evaluating issues and ideas Thinking; IX. Creative-thinking skills

Moreover, we often work harder for people we like, admire, and see as role models (Lickona, 1991).

During the interview we ask applicants about their non-school related interests to gauge what they value in life and how passionately they speak about their family, friends, and hobbies. We also give them real-life classroom scenarios to think about. This not only gives us an idea whether the applicant can think on their feet, which is a skill all teachers must have, but

Table 12.2. Similarities between HoM, Building Blocks of Character, IBLP Traits, and ATL Skills

Habits of Mind	Building Blocks of Character	IB Learner Profile Traits	ATL Skill Category, Cluster, and Indicator (IB)
8. Persisting	Performance		Self-Management; IV. Affective • Managing state of mind • Perseverance
9. Managing impulsivity	Performance	Balance	Self-Management; IV. Affective • Managing state of mind Emotional management
10. Listening with understanding and empathy	Performance Moral	Caring, open-minded	Social; II. Collaboration skills • Working effectively with others • Practice empathy • Listen actively to other perspectives and ideas
11. Thinking flexibly	Intellectual	Caring, open-minded, thinker, inquirer	Thinking; VIII. Critical-thinking skills • Analyzing and evaluating issues and ideas Thinking; IX. Creative-thinking skills • Practice flexible thinking
12. Thinking about thinking	Intellectual Moral	Reflective, caring	Self-Management; V. Reflection skills • (Re) considering the process of learning; choosing and using ATL skills
13. Striving for accuracy	Performance Moral	Principled, caring, knowledgeable	Research; VI. Information Literacy • Collect, record and verify data
14. Questioning and posing problems	Intellectual	Inquirers	Thinking; VIII. Critical-thinking skills • Analyzing and evaluating issues and ideas Thinking; IX. Creative-thinking skills

may be even more important is how the candidate will respond to the scenario, that is, the moral dilemma.

Some candidates want to know what the school rules are or even what consequences the school will allow them to issue, as they want to show compliance with the school's behavior management policy. While others ask questions about the class, an individual student, and other matters as they want to grasp the context. They often do this verbalizing which action they

Table 12.3. Similarities between HoM, Building Blocks of Character, IBLP Traits, and ATL Skills

Habits of Mind	Building Blocks of Character	IB Learner Profile Traits	ATL Skill Category, Cluster, and Indicator (IB)
14. Finding humor	Intellectual	Communicator	Creative thinking. IX: Generating novel ideas and considering new perspectives • Make guesses, ask "what if" questions and generate testable hypotheses
15. Thinking	Intellectual Performance	Caring	Collaboration: II. Working effectively with others. • Delegate and share responsibility for decision-making
16. Remaining open to continuous learning	Intellectual Performance	Lifelong learners	Development of all skills.

Summary: Character education and the habits of mind are similar as they both aim to prepare students to live successfully and make ethical decisions.

consider best. These candidates are mindful about conflicting virtues (such as loyalty and honesty or fairness and respect) and often unknowingly show moral reasoning and practical wisdom. We prefer the teacher guided by virtue ethics over those who favor a more outdated moral theory of deontology or utilitarianism.

Becoming a school of character also meant that we need to provide teachers with continuous professional development. We provide regular in-house workshops for staff on character education and expect that all new staff complete the online Leading Character Education in Schools course from the Jubilee Centre before they join the school. Furthermore, we have made a commitment to offer (virtual) workshops provided by the Association for Character Education. Resources are regularly updated and made available electronically and in the school library for teachers to consult.

Although character education was initially driven by the school leadership team, it is inspiring to see that a more organic development is taking place as a group of teachers started a character education work group in which they propose, develop, and implement new character education initiatives within subjects and across the school. More teachers are joining this group as they are becoming more aware of the importance of virtue development in their students.

These teachers are starting to think more deeply about the strategies to cultivate teaching with character development in mind. Besides developing our teachers, we also offer parent information sessions and have a home-school wellbeing committee to include parents in our character education implementation efforts. Our aim is to have a home-school partnership in which all parents contribute to the caught, taught and sought aspects (Jubilee Centre, 2017, p. 9) of the school's character education program.

Summary: Implementing character education at JBS was initiated by the school's leaders but is now embraced by the school community.

CHARACTER EDUCATION IS CAUGHT, TAUGHT, AND SOUGHT

Although the distinction of character caught, taught, and sought makes it easier for schools to design, implement and evaluate their character education curriculum, the approaches overlap and must be seen in tandem (Berkowitz, 2021; Harrison et al., 2016b; Watts et al., 2021).

Caught Curriculum

We already mentioned "the hidden curriculum" which is present in every school and has according to Arthur (2003) a bigger impact on student behavior than the taught curriculum. The ethos of all schools is value driven and consequently these values are caught by the students in the school. We also addressed the importance of the role of the "good" teacher so students can emulate their character.

Character education and HoM have much in common in this regard. Moreover, both approaches have high expectations of their students (and rightly so), and students and teachers speak the same virtue language or HoM language allowing for a commitment to excellence across the programs. As a result, the students feel motivated and inspired by their teachers and the positive ethos of their school.

Taught Curriculum

Whilst a part of the school ethos is caught by the students, another part must be explicitly taught. Berkowitz (2021), Harrison et al. (2016b), Kristjánsson (2015), and Lickona (1991) promote a character development model which is based on the head, heart and hand (i.e. moral knowing, moral feeling and moral acting). As mentioned before this means that students must know the virtue or skill, be aware or feel the emotion to apply the skill and then act upon it (i.e., virtue knowledge, virtue reasoning, and virtue practice).

Teaching character strengths can be done as a discrete or stand-alone subject (such as the mandated Moral Education course in the UAE) or through and within other subjects such as English, humanities, math, science, and PHE. The intellectual virtues will be at the heart of the taught curriculum, whilst "the moral, civic and performance virtues can enhance and enrich the teaching of the curriculum because of the opportunities they provide for understanding academic learning in its relational (moral), social (civic) and performance contexts" (Harrison et al., 2016, p. 66).

These are all opportunities provided by the school to support character development. This can range from after-school activities related to sports, drama, arts, and environmental clubs to the school council as well as students attending school trips and camps. An important component of the sought curriculum and especially so in IB schools is the opportunity to be involved in service-learning activities which can range from raising awareness for a good cause to giving up time to volunteer and help others. The above are all excellent ways to develop character virtues—mostly performance, moral, and civic (Watts et al., 2021)

Are We There Yet?

All educators know that learning is a lifelong journey. It is therefore no surprise, that although we embarked on our character education journey a few years ago, we are not there yet. *Eudaimonia* or flourishing is a lifelong activity and so there is no final destination. We constantly strive to be better in all we do as we feel that we have a moral obligation to our students to prepare them for life so they can truly flourish.

Although it is important to evaluate the impact of our activities and interventions, we also feel this is not an easy task; as how would one measure virtue? Are our students becoming more compassionate, more inquisitive, and more resilient? It is hard to tell as we have no proper measurement tool. However, we have seen attendance and punctuality improve over the past years. Notwithstanding the pandemic, the DSWC and PASS data have shown upward trends in several areas: improved student-teacher relationships, a more positive school climate and a decrease in all four bullying domains (i.e., verbal, physical, social, and cyber).

Moreover, teachers report less behavior management concerns, and we also feel that these incidents have become less serious in nature. We hear that older student are starting to correct the behavior of younger students in public spaces in the school which seems to indicate that respect, integrity and courage are more activated. We also see an increase in students' interest to apply for leadership positions and there is an uptake of student led initiatives to improve school life. These initiatives range from student led assemblies to organizing awareness campaigns, themed days, and school spirit days.

Although our external student achievement data was very good in 2020 and 2021, we feel that it is too early to assess whether our character education efforts have made a positive impact. It is hard to pinpoint whether all "the above positives" are the result of our consciously planned and implemented character education program or whether other forces were at play.

The Jubilee Centre's *Character Education Evaluation Handbook for Schools* (Harrison et al., 2016a) has helped in some ways to formatively assess our program. However, this was externally carried out by the Association for Character Education. As a result, JBS proudly attained as the first school outside the UK the Kitemark Award in November 2020.

Summary: The development and implementation of a conscious planned character education program at JBS is making a positive impact on school climate but more research is needed.

SUMMARY

As we begin to recover from the COVID-19 crisis we hope this chapter allows the reader to reflect on their school's approach to teaching and learning. We feel that there is an opportunity now to show courage by leaving the era of instrumentalist education behind us and embark on a journey which allows us—teachers and students—to flourish. Selecting the right navigation system is in the hands of school leaders who based on personal experience and practice, proper information collection, and reflection have an opportunity to act in the best interest of their students.

As Martin Luther King Jr. said, "Intelligence plus character—that is the goal of true education." Therefore, the HoM and Character Education have a place in every good school preparing their students to be successful, while in the now and in the future.

REFERENCES

Anderson, J. C. (2008). Habits of mind: A journey of continuous growth. In A. L. Costa and B. Kallick (Eds.), *Learning and leading with habits of mind: Essential characteristics for success* (pp. 59–68). Alexandria: ASCD.

Aristotle. (2004). *The Nicomachean ethics.* London: Penguin Books.

Arthur, J. (2003). *Education with character. The moral economy of schooling.* London: RoutledgeFalmer.

Arthur, J. (2016). *Is grit the magic elixir of good character? Some reflections on Angela Duckworth's new book, GRIT: The power of passion and persever-ance.* Retrieved from Insight Series: https://www.jubileecentre.ac.uk/userfiles /jubileecentre/pdf/insight-series/Is_Grit_the_Magic_Elixir_of_Good_Character _InsightSeries2016.pdf

Arthur, J. (2017). *Teaching character and virtue in schools.* Oxfordshire: Routledge.

Berkowitz, M. W. (2021). *Primed for character education. Six design principles for school improvement.* New York: Routledge.

Brooks, D. (2015). *The road to character.* Penguin Random House.

Columbus, C. (Director). (1990). *Home alone* [Motion Picture].

Costa, A. L. (2008). Describing the habits of mind. In A. L. Costa and B. Kallick (Eds.), *Learning and leading with Habits of Mind: 16 essential characteristics for success* (pp. 15–41). Alexandria: ASCD.

Costa, A. L., & Kallick, B. (2008). Habits of Mind in the curriculum. In A. L. Costa and B. Kallick (Eds.), *Learning and leading with Habits of Mind: 16 essential characteristics for success* (pp. 42–58). Alexandria: ASCD.

Duckworth, A. (2016). *Grit: The power of passion and perseverance.* London: Vermilion.

Dweck, C. (2006). *Mindset. Changing the way you think to fulfil your potential.* New York: Robinson.

Gleason, D. (2017). *At what cost? Defending adolescent development in fiercely com-petitive schools.* Developmental Empathy LLC.

Harrison. (2016). *Teaching character in the primary classroom.* London: Sage.

Harrison, T., Arthur, J., & Burn, E. (2016a). *Character education evaluation hand-book for schools.* Retrieved from University of Birmingham, Jubilee Centre for Character and Virtues: https://www.jubileecentre.ac.uk/1721/character-education

Harrison, T., Morris, I., & Ryan, J. (2016b). *Teaching character education in the primary classroom.* London: Sage.

Jubilee Centre for Character and Virtues. (2015). *Statement on teacher education and character education.* Retrieved from Univeristy of Birmingham, Jubilee Centre for Character and Virtues: https://www.jubileecentre.ac.uk/userfiles/jubileecentre/pdf/ character-education/Statement_on_Teacher_Education_and_Character_Education .pdf

Jubilee Centre for Character and Virtues. (2017). *A framework for character educa-tion in schools.* Retrieved from A Framework for Character Education: https://www .jubileecentre.ac.uk/userfiles/jubileecentre/pdf/character-education/Framework %20for%20Character%20Education.pdf

Kristjánsson, K. (2015). *Aristotelian character education.* Oxon: Routledge Taylor and Francis Group.

Lickona, T. (1991). *Educating for character: How our schools can teach respect and responsibility.* New York: Bantam Books.

Lickona, T. (1997). The teacher's role in character education. *The Journal of Education,* 63–80.

Loewus, L. (2021). *Why teachers leave—or don't: A look at the numbers.* Retrieved from Education Week: https://www.edweek.org/teaching-learning/why-teachers-leave-or-dont-a-look-at-the-numbers/2021/05

Martin-Kniep, G. O., & Kallick, B. (2021). *Do you want ALL students to flourish and develop their full potential?* Retrieved from ckarchive: https://ckarchive.com/b/qdu8h7hkzqqw

OECD. (2015). Retrieved from oecd.org: https://www.oecd.org/education/A-Strategic-Approach-to-Education-and%20Skills-Policies-for-the-United-Arab-Emirates.pdf

Robinson, K., & Aronica, L. (2015). *Creative schools: The grassroots revolution that's transforming education.* New York: Viking.

Schwartz, B., & Sharpe, K. (2010). *Practical wisdom: The right way to do the right thing.* New York: Penguin Group.

Ted. (2006). *Sir Ken Robinson. Do schools kill creativity?* Retrieved from Ted2006: https://www.ted.com/talks/sir_ken_robinson_do_schools_kill_creativity

Tough, P. (2012). *How children succeed: Grit, curiosity, and the hidden power of character.* New York: First Mariner Books.

Unesco. (2021). *Teachers.* Retrieved from Unesco: https://en.unesco.org/themes/teachers

Wagner, T. (2008). *The global achievement gap: Why even our best schools don't teach the new survival skills our children need—and what we can do about it.* New York: Basic Books.

Wagner, T., & Dintersmith, T. (2015). *Most likely to succeed: Preparing our kids for the innovation era.* New York: Scribner.

Watts, P., Fullard, M., & Peterson, A. (2021). *Understanding character education.* London: Open University Press.

Chapter 13

The Convergence of Special Education and Habits of Mind

Daniel L. Vollrath

Picture this: It is the beginning of August. Summer has provided you with much-needed R & R. Over the summer, you may have found yourself *finding wonderment and awe* in the simple act of relaxation, or through *managing your impulsivity* by basking in the sun. Perhaps you spent time *remaining open to continuous learning* by taking adventuresome trips with family and friends, or *thinking flexibly* by creating time-consuming summertime meals you would not dare to make during the school year.

While these dog days of summer are not officially over, you recognize that young minds yearning for knowledge will be barreling into your classroom in the near future. Furthermore, *metacognition* might be settling in for you—thoughts, questions, feelings, and ideas—about what your upcoming classroom will look like, feel like, and sound like.

Now, fast forward your thinking to the last few days of summer before the start of your new school year. This is time to view your classroom rosters, ask yourself and colleagues questions about certain students, and speculate about information or concerns you might need to be aware of, such as: Who has an IEP? Who has a 504 plan? What are some behaviors I need to be mindful of? How will I accommodate certain students? Who needs special accommodations? Who are my neurodivergent learners?

Finally, the first day of school has arrived. You are front and center in the classroom staring at 22 students. That habit of metacognition you performed back in August, and those questions you contemplated a couple of days ago, were now helpful in providing you with a base for understanding your new group of students.

Many of you reading this chapter may be able to relate to this type of thought process leading up to a new school year. As teachers, no matter how much preparation goes into planning, the following through of those plans can change at any moment. Furthermore, as teachers, it is important to recognize your students who learn differently. These diverse learners must be provided with all the necessary accommodations and supports to be successful. Students with learning disabilities must never be left behind in their learning; instead, teachers should do all they can to offer strategies for building productive behaviors within the learning environment.

This chapter is designed to introduce teachers to Habits of Mind through a special education lens. Special education can be viewed in a myriad of ways depending on one's experience, understanding, and what it looks like within the learning environment. In this chapter, I will describe certain learning disabilities that I have recognized through my experience of being a classroom teacher. Furthermore, I will explain how Habits of Mind can impact and serve importance toward improving certain behaviors associated with students with learning disabilities.

LEARNING DISABILITIES AND HABITS OF MIND

Consider the following story, which took place within Mr. E's English classroom:

Throughout Mr. E's PowerPoint to his English class, Lucas, a student in the class, continued interrupting by shouting out comments and talking to peers. Understanding that Lucas had been diagnosed with dyslexia, Mr. E. wanted to further support Lucas's ability to self-manage some of his disruptive behaviors. Here is a summary of Mr. E's discussion with Lucas after class:

Lucas and I discussed his impulsive behavior and ways to self-manage it. Together we brainstormed and decided to try two different strategies: waiting three seconds before calling out, and writing down what you want to say instead of interrupting. I acknowledged that these were great ways to manage his impulsivity. We wrote down these strategies and placed them on his desk as a reminder.

The story above demonstrates how the Habits of Mind can be integrated into daily instruction for students with specific learning disabilities. In this scenario, Lucas learned to integrate the habit of *managing impulsivity* by waiting a few seconds, writing down what he wants to say before being called on, and not interrupting.

In a later follow-up discussion, Mr. E. had explained that using these strategies with Lucas has increased his focus in classroom. In addition, Mr. E. found that *managing impulsivity* had a positive effect with all his students. *Managing impulsivity* became part of the classroom vocabulary and had an authentic use within the learning environment. Mr. E. claims that many of his students are now more mindful with displaying this habit within the classroom. For instance, when trying to settle down students before the start of a discussion, Mr. E. might say "Let's all take a moment to manage our impulsivity before moving forward."

What Is a Specific Learning Disability?

A specific learning disability is "a disorder in one or more of the basic psychological processes involved in understanding or in using language, spoken or written that may manifest itself in the imperfect ability to listen, think, speak, read, write, spell, or do mathematical equations" (IDEA, 2004). Students with a specific learning disability may have related conditions that present themselves in ways that also qualify for special education supports and services.

Below is a list of specific learning disabilities and related disorders. In addition, provided are examples of strategies that incorporate certain Habits of Mind when working with students with learning disabilities. This list comprises the most commonly recognized disabilities and disorders within the classroom setting.

Specific learning disabilities:

- Dyslexia
- Dysgraphia
- Auditory process disorder

Related disorders:

- Attention deficit hyperactivity disorder (ADHD)
- Executive functioning

Specific Learning Disabilities

Dyslexia

The idea that reading comes naturally to all children is a commonly held assumption (Shaywitz, 2003). Children with dyslexia often present difficulties in consistently performing skills related to phonological awareness, decoding, fluency, vocabulary, and comprehension (Mercer, Mercer, & Pullen, 2011). Schools often have specific academic programs and teachers who work with students with dyslexia and other reading disabilities. The practice of building reading habits can be useful in strengthening students' perseverance, resilience, and overall skills and comprehension.

In 2012, Zielinski and colleagues implemented a spelling intervention with three students diagnosed with a learning disability in written language (a symptom of dyslexia). The "Cover, Copy, Compare (CCC)" strategy was implemented over 20 sessions within a high school resource room. This CCC strategy begins with copying a word while looking at the correct spelling, followed by covering the word along with the copied word, writing the word from memory, and lastly, comparing the three versions.

If all three words match, then students move to the next word; if not, they copy the incorrectly spelled word three more times. The results of the study indicated that this intervention increased spelling performance overtime for these students (Zielinski et al., 2012). Students in the study were receptive to the intervention, which allowed them to think flexibly, strive for accuracy, and employ persistence with guidance from their teacher.

Although students with dyslexia and related learning disabilities each have unique strengths and challenges, integrating specific Habits of Mind can provide critical dispositional support to sustain perseverance. Here are some specific examples of how a teacher might lead these discussions with students.

Implementation with Habits of Mind and Dyslexia:

1. Thinking Flexibly: Brainstorm different strategies with students that may work in supporting their academic needs. For example, ask students, "How can we work together in accomplishing the goal of comprehending reading passages?" Consider options, such as colored paper and fonts that may be more dyslexia-friendly; creative graphic organizers to support specific comprehension strategies; or visual and auditory texts. Offer opportunities for students to make suggestions, try new strategies, and reinforce the habit of thinking flexibly.
2. Taking Responsible Risks: Reading out loud can conjure up anxiety and frustration for students with dyslexia. To ease student tension, provide an informal notification that next class he/she will be reading out loud. This reminder can hopefully take away the element of surprise, and provide student opportunity to build confidence in persisting. Additionally, it is important to provide the student with the passage and possible follow-up questions to consider. Giving students this opportunity will help facilitate safe and responsible risk taking.

Dysgraphia

One of the most essential skills in school and life is the ability to write coherently. Dysgraphia is a brain-based disorder that causes students trouble with expressing their thoughts in writing, with obvious detrimental effects on academic progress and performance (Fuchs, Mock, Morgan, & Young, 2003). It is estimated that about 7 to 15 percent of the general education student population has dysgraphia (Döhla, Willmes, & Heim, 2018).

Difficulty with organizing and writing cohesive text is not something that students with dysgraphia alone struggle with—many students with and without learning disabilities often have difficulty with these tasks (Dunn, 2013). The following two Habits of Mind examples provides specific techniques to support writing for students with dysgraphia.

Implementation with Habits of Mind and Dysgraphia:

1. Taking Responsible Risks: Suggest trying different approaches that might assist in writing success. Offer paper with raised lines for accuracy, practice taking notes and then comparing with teacher-generated notes, consider various technologies that employ speech-to-text writing options, and recommend more mobile and adequate writing grips (thicker pencils, etc.).

2. Persisting: Enforce the habit of persisting when working with a student with dysgraphia. The process of writing may bring forth anxiety, frustration, and temptation to quit; it is important to stress persisting in these tasks. Consider the option of utilizing a goal sheet with specific steps to complete during the writing process. Furthermore, offer small rewards and incentives for achieving writing goals.

Auditory Processing Disorder

Children with an auditory processing disorder (APD) typically have issues with processing and making meaning of sounds. For example, if a teacher presenting information about narrative writing states, "Narrative writing is any kind of writing that tells a story," a student with APD might interpret this statement as, "Narrow writing is a kind story that tells rights." The student may hear the words from their teacher; although, the actual processing and comprehension might not be fully interpreted. Here are some examples of using the Habits of Mind with students with APD.

Implementation with Habits of Mind and Auditory Processing:

1. Questioning and Posing Problems: Communicate with the student about the importance of being a questioning and problem-posing learner. Encourage the student who looks for problems to solve through collaboration with others. This is an opportunity to explain self-advocacy and take the steps to figure things out when confusion arises. Asking the teacher to repeat instructions, rephrase, and clarify ideas are all great examples of using this habit to enhance learning.
2. Applying Past Knowledge to New Situations: Ask the question, "What past knowledge about your learning can you use to support yourself in this new learning situation?" A simple conversation about past practices and strategies that may have worked for a student in their prior classes could elicit a wealth of knowledge for a teacher. Consider including visuals, written explanations, study guides, and hands-on activities in instruction.

Related Disorders

Attention Deficit Hyperactivity Disorder (ADHD)

Attention deficit hyperactivity disorder (ADHD) is a behavioral disorder affecting millions of children in the United States every year (National Institute of Mental Health, 2022). The signs of ADHD include consistent patterns of distractibility and/or hyperactivity that typically interferes with functioning in multiple environments (Hamilton & Astramovich, 2016). For students with ADHD, many times when an answer cannot immediately be known, the habit of giving up or writing down any answer may occur (Costa & Kallick, 2008, p.18).

Often students with attention deficits are easily distracted, inattentive, hyperactive, impulsive, and lack problem-solving skills, which in turn can cause a lack of academic success and frustration for students and teachers alike (Shillingford-Butler & Theodore, 2013).

Implementation of the Habits of Mind and ADHD:

1. Striving for Accuracy: Put emphasis on the idea of not giving up. Promote this habit to the whole class by having groups of students generate scenarios about how completing a task inaccurately can have negative effects on the outcome. This activity could serve as an example

for a student with ADHD to refer back to when confronted with a challenging task.

2. Thinking about Thinking (Metacognition): Discuss the significance of being aware of your thoughts, feelings, intentions, and actions in life. Collaborate about ways that might assist in being mindful of your actions and how those action can affect others. Consider coping mechanisms and modeling ways to be metacognitive. For instance, being more aware of how you could calm down after an argument with a peer. One might find that taking a minute to focus on their breathing could relieve anxiety and get them to calm.

Executive Functioning Deficits

For students with learning disabilities, executive functioning skills can play an integral role in their success. For children with executive functioning issues, difficulties are present in the ability to manage impulsivity, regulate emotions, think flexibly, store information in working memory, self-monitor, plan and prioritize, initiate tasks, and organize themselves and their worlds.

The model of a funnel is used to help explain the executive learning process for both successful and unsuccessful students (Meltzer, 2007): "When students are able to use the processes of executive functioning, they are able to coordinate (or funnel) the various tasks and skills required to complete their work; however, when students struggle to coordinate these tasks and skills, the funnel becomes blocked, and they are unable to reflect work that reflects their abilities" (p.80).

Implementation of Habits of Mind for Executive Functioning:

1. Remaining Open to Continuous Learning: Discuss with students the idea of being open to learning how to become more organized. Work with students on brainstorming ways to continuously learn and build upon their "bag of tricks" in managing their workload in school. Try new strategies, and if they don't work, try something else.

2. Taking Responsible Risks: Similar to the habit of remaining open to continuous learning, students should also realize that in order to succeed they need to try new things that might not resemble strategies, techniques, or methods they have used in the past. Students may experiment with software, both in computer format and on smartphone devices. By experimenting, students may learn better ways to plan, organize, and remember important tasks.

SAMPLE STUDENT CASES

As an educator, one of the most important tools for planning instruction is knowing your students. Often this process takes time and interaction with students in and outside of the classroom. Recognizing personalities, strengths, weaknesses, and learning styles of students allows for effective teacher-student relationships to blossom.

For students with a learning disability, it is important for teachers to know information about them prior to the beginning of the school year. This process normally starts with the teacher reviewing a student's IEP. Within this document is information that can provide insights into the prospective learning and performance of a particular child with a learning disability. In reviewing the IEP, teachers can begin to plan approaches to support a student's annual goals, objectives, and implement necessary supports to ensure student success.

In this section, I will present case samples of particular students with an IEP. In addition, the focus will connect to the student's areas of need, as presented in their IEP. These particular case samples should offer ideas and strategies on how to begin thinking about integrating the Habits of Mind into inclusive learning settings, resource room contexts, and most importantly, students with learning disabilities.

After describing each student and his/her strengths and challenges, a list of relevant Habits of Mind to consider will be presented. Additionally, a discussion of how these Habits of Mind might be integrated into instruction will follow.

Keep in mind that the Habits of Mind presented in each scenario are ones believed to be a natural fit given the learning contexts. However, those who know the student best could determine which habit might be more appropriate than others. As you read each scenario, think about what Habits of Mind might work for your student(s) and how they could be addressed in a classroom and/or across different learning environmental settings.

Scenario #1

Background

Gregory is a fifth-grade student who has been diagnosed with dysgraphia. Often his writing is disorganized, and he struggles with writing expression. In addition, Gregory was diagnosed with ADHD in the fourth grade. ADHD has affected his ability to stay organized, focused, and on-task. His parents believe that Gregory's issues at home carry over into the educational environment. Both parents feel Gregory needs to self-advocate, take on more self-responsibility, and be held accountable for his decisions.

While Gregory is a polite young man with an outgoing personality, he tends to distract himself and others during instructional time in the classroom. This seems to have caused more frequent disciplinary issues with Gregory, which has exacerbated academic difficulties.

Teacher Reports

Gregory's history teacher presents him as a student with the ability to work and share ideas with the class. He struggles with abstract concepts and completing assignments. Overall, Gregory wants to do well on his assignments, although Gregory does not put a lot of effort into completing his work.

Gregory's science teacher states that he volunteers to answer questions in class; although, he does this by shouting out answers and not giving others an opportunity to participate. His work completion is inconsistent. Gregory starts many assignments but does not complete them. Gregory enjoys sharing ideas, providing insight, and shows interest within the class yet often digresses. Gregory has not shown a lot of motivation and ability within the course.

Habits of Mind

After a month into the school year, Gregory's English teacher recognized the issues presented in his IEP documentation were accurate to his current observed behavior and academic performance. The English teacher took into consideration the problems that were occurring and decided to employ a Habits of Mind strategy to address some of the difficulties that Gregory was experiencing. The Habits of Mind selected by the teacher were: taking responsible risks, managing impulsivity, striving for accuracy, and thinking and communicating with clarity and precision. Here are how these Habits of Mind would support Gregory:

- Taking responsible risks: Gregory would seem to benefit from taking responsible risks to assist with his dysgraphia. As the teacher, it would be important to stress the idea of taking responsible risks by trying different approaches within writing assignments.
- Managing impulsivity: Gregory's ADHD seems to have affected not only himself but other students in the class. One approach to support this issue is to develop a self-monitoring plan with Gregory. Explain to Gregory the importance of what self-monitoring looks like, feels like, sounds like, and how it connects to managing your impulsivity.

- Striving for accuracy: Difficulties with staying organized is an area addressed in Gregory's IEP. Presenting Gregory with a routine—a paper or electronic folder system—will support him and his teachers in monitoring his organization and work progress. This process will ultimately help Gregory stay on track. It is essential to review this strategy and make any necessary revisions with Gregory on a consistent basis.
- Thinking and communicating with clarity and precision: Recognizing that Gregory enjoys communicating and speaking out loud with classmates is a positive attribute. However, it seems as though his thoughts are not conveyed clearly. One habit to stress with Gregory is the ability to communicate with clear language. For instance, model the practice of speaking slower and with more concision. Or, create opportunities where Gregory can speak with peers and focus on pausing between his thoughts and ideas.

Once the four Habits of Mind above are contemplated, designed, and mapped out to fit Gregory's particular educational and behavioral needs, the process of monitoring is then put into effect. Since Gregory will be matriculating into middle school in a year, it is important to instill responsibility and the opportunity to self-manage. Gregory will be encouraged to self-monitor the habits of *taking responsible risks* and *striving for accuracy*.

To assist in this endeavor, Gregory will keep a Habits of Mind self-monitoring plan (see below) to evaluate his work with these two Habits of Mind. Being that both dispositions are more internal, and not easily observable from an outsider's point of view, the self-monitoring plan will help guide Gregory's consistency in becoming more mindful and reflective.

As for *managing impulsivity* and *thinking and communicating with clarity and precision*, Gregory and his teacher will take a team approach. In this case, the teacher and Gregory will first discuss what these habits should and should not look like in the classroom. Together they will create a list and discuss examples of when these habits should be used.

Once Gregory and his teacher generate a list, together they will create a non-verbal signal that will serve as a reminder to change the behavior. For example, when Gregory decides to interrupt with a comment on a fellow student's presentation, the teacher will tap once on Gregory's desk. This will hopefully trigger Gregory's ability to manage his impulsivity. Instead of interrupting, Gregory will write down his comments on paper to discuss when the presentation is finished.

Habits of Mind Self-Monitoring Plan

Gregory Self-Monitoring Plan

Every Friday, Gregory will evaluate his behaviors in reference to the two Habits of Mind: *taking responsible risks* and *striving for accuracy*. This will be completed by means of a rating scale, as follows: 1 (never), 2 (a little bit), 3 (half of the week), 4 (almost every day), 5 (used every day).

Taking Responsible Risks: Willing to take calculated and responsible risks by trying different approaches in writing.

Never	A little bit	Half of the week	Almost every-day	Used everyday
1	2	3	4	5

Evidence:

Striving for Accuracy: Greg will strive for accuracy to stay organized, follow a daily routine, stay on track with assignments and due dates, and find ways to improve constantly in English class.

Never	A little bit	Half of the week	Almost every-day	Used everyday
1	2	3	4	5

Evidence:

Scenario #2

Background

Sean is an incoming high school freshman. He is diagnosed with Autism Level 1, meaning he has support needs related to social skills and dealing with the day-to-day functioning in the classroom. Sean's least restrictive environment for learning has been determined to be general education, college prep track, with in-class support related to his IEP.

Sean tends to be set in his ways and exhibits resistance to learning alternative viewpoints. In the classroom, Sean disturbs others by poking and touching them, making inappropriate noises, and conducting himself inappropriately for attention. These behaviors have hindered his ability to work successfully with peers. This is a major concern for all of his teachers since many of the classroom activities incorporate small group work. Expressing feelings, thoughts, and ideas are especially difficult for Sean due to his lack of personal awareness and communication skills.

Teacher Reports

Sean's history teacher reports that he is impressed with Sean's ability to recall events in detail and provide facts and figures when needed. He has a positive outlook and shows an interest and desire to learn. Sean's view of the world and history, however, tends to be limited. He has a difficult time with role-playing activities and tasks which require considering other points of view. Although other students in the class respect Sean for knowing factual content, they are starting to become hesitant to work with him due to distracting actions and argumentative comments.

Sean's math teacher reports that he completes almost all homework assignments, and the answers are usually correct. It was noted on a few occasions by Sean's mom that he was awake doing homework past midnight because his perception was, "If I don't finish all the problems, and get them all correct, my teacher will be mad at me." When other students are solving problems on the board, Sean will moan, bang his fists, or comment if the writing isn't the neatest, not large enough, or has errors. This is beginning to disturb the class and the teacher is afraid it will cause some students to stop volunteering.

Habits of Mind

After speaking with Sean's counselor, case manager, and other classroom teachers, Sean's history teacher aligned Sean's IEP information with specific Habits of Mind. The goal was to create a plan to support Sean in using appropriate social skills during class. The Habits of Mind selected by the teacher were: listening and understanding with empathy, thinking interdependently, thinking flexibly, and applying past knowledge to new situations.

- Listening and understanding with empathy: A big part of Sean's issues stems from him not reacting well to other students. If he disagrees with a viewpoint, or thinks someone is incorrect, it would be valuable for Sean to think about the impact his comments make on others feelings and confidence.
- Thinking interdependently: A school's role is to prepare all students for life beyond high school, where the norm is to have people working together in a respectful and productive manner. Sean needs to develop this disposition, not request to work alone, or alienate himself from the group by his negative interactions.
- Thinking flexibly: This habit is essential for Sean to develop as he moves through high school and beyond, especially since his autism causes him to think in only black or white. His current thinking—related to a historical fact—won't allow him to predict how life in the United

States would be different today if the South had won the Civil War. Sean can't get past the fact that the South *didn't* win. If he is to fully develop as a student, and have success in school and life, he needs to be able to look at scenarios in a different way and consider alternate viewpoints.

- Applying past knowledge to new situations: Sean is a concrete learner with a very good memory. History can be viewed as an entertaining story of our past. However, if the goal is to apply past successes and failures to present and future scenarios, Sean will continue to struggle. It is important that Sean receive extensive practice at "what if" cases and begin to predict how past knowledge can be beneficial in new situations.

Once the four Habits of Mind above were contemplated, designed, and mapped out to fit Sean's particular educational and behavioral needs, the process of monitoring was put into effect. A Habits of Mind guided-monitoring plan (see below) will serve as an opportunity for Sean to reflect, along with the guidance and feedback from his teacher. Every two weeks, Sean and his teacher will meet to review and complete the guided monitoring plan.

For the habit of *listening and understanding with empathy*, the teacher will talk with Sean before class about treating his peers with respect during presentations and in group work settings. Tapping on the head of a tiger stuffed animal—the class mascot—will be a signal from the teacher to reinforce Sean that he needs to be kind to others as they are speaking, and refrain from making rude comments.

For the habit of *thinking interdependently*, the teacher will meet with Sean briefly the day before a group project or a collaborative activity. This will give Sean a day's notice to think of ideas and feel more comfortable joining a group. In order to help Sean better develop the habit of *thinking flexibly* and *applying past knowledge to new situations,* the teacher will keep Sean informed a day ahead of time in reference to: gaining his perspective on prior knowledge in regard to specific content, figuring out how he will handle activities for the upcoming class, and what he could do differently to make American history class more beneficial for him and peers.

Habits of Mind Guided-Monitoring Plan

Sean Guided-Monitoring Plan

Every two weeks, Sean will meet with his history teacher to discuss and evaluate progress made towards meeting his outlined Habits of Mind goals. The teacher will ask questions to Sean orally and record his responses in a journal.

1. Was there any time during the last two weeks in class where you believe you used *Listening and understanding with empathy*? When did this occur? Give an example.
2. Was there any time during the last two weeks in class where you believe you used *Thinking interdependently*? When did this occur? Give an example.
3. Was there any time during the last two weeks in class where you believe you used *Thinking flexibly*? When did this occur? Give an example.
4. Was there any time during the last two weeks in class where you believe you used *Applying past knowledge to new situations*? When did this occur? Give an example.

The teacher will compare Sean's responses with any anecdotal evidence recorded, or any mental notes made during the same time frame.

SUMMARY

Habits of Mind can be integrated into daily instruction and progress monitoring in a variety of ways. While there is no set procedure or protocol for when or where to reference habits, teaching them explicitly and referencing them consistently can truly make a difference.

One way to start with the Habits of Mind might be by using the language. Instead of using phrases such as "remain on task," "try your best," or "don't quit," try replacing those phrases with "manage your impulsivity," "let's strive for accuracy," or "persist until you are done." Simple statements with Habits of Mind offer more intention and meaning behind the behaviors you want your students—with learning disabilities and without learning disabilities—to display on a consistent basis.

In this chapter, the Habits of Mind have been directed toward students with learning disabilities; although it should be noted that *all* students and teachers can benefit from being reminded to use these beneficial and success-oriented dispositions.

Now that you have read this chapter, what Habits of Mind might be most helpful for your students with learning disabilities? Or, what Habits of Mind could all of your students benefit from within your classroom?

REFERENCES

Costa, A. L., & Kallick, B. (2008). *Learning and leading with habits of mind: 16 essential characteristics for success.* Alexandria, VA: ASCD.

Döhla, D., Willmes, K., & Heim, S. (2018). Cognitive profiles of developmental dys-graphia. *Frontiers in Psychology, 9*(2006), 1–12. doi: 10.3389/fpsyg.2018.02006

Dunn, M. (2013). Using art media during pre-writing: Helping students with dys-graphia manage idea generation before encoding text. *Exceptionality, 21*(4), 224–237. doi: 10.1080/09362835.2013.802234

Fuchs, D., Mock, D., Morgan, P., & Young, C. (2003). Responsiveness-to-instruction: Definitions, evidence, and implications for learning disabilities construct. *Learning Disabilities Research & Practice, 18*(3), 157–171.

Hamilton, N. J., & Astramovich, R. L. (2016). Teaching strategies for students with ADHD: Findings from the field. *Education, 136*(4).

Harold S. Koplewicz, MD. (2016). Child Mind Institute, Care Education Science. https://childmind.org/bio/harold-s-koplewicz-md/

Individuals with Disabilities Education Act, 20 U.S.C. § 1400 (2004).

Meltzer, L. (2007). *Executive functioning in education: From theory to practice.* New York, NY: Guildford Press.

Mercer, C. D., Mercer, A., & Pullen, P. C. (2011). *Teaching students with learning problems* (8th ed). Upper Saddle River, NJ: Pearson.

National Institute of Mental Health (2022). Attention-Deficit/Hyperactivity Disorder. Retrieved June 29, 2022, from: https://www.nimh.nih.gov/health/topics/attention -deficit-hyperactivity-disorder-adhd

Shaywitz, S. (2003). *Overcoming dyslexia.* New York, NY: Vintage Books.

Shillingford-Butler, M. A., & Theodore, L. (2013). Students diagnosed with atten-tion deficit hyperactivity disorder: Collaborative strategies for school counselors. *Professional School Counseling, 16*(4), 235–244. doi: 10.1111/jsr.12049

Chapter 14

Assessing Habits of Mind

James Anderson

In 2008, Costa and Kallick discuss the topic of assessing the Habits of Mind in Part III of *Learning and Leading with Habits of Mind*. They wrote: "There is great value in making the Habits of Mind explicit with indicators that guide us in observing growth and improvement. Assessment provides a measure of that developmental growth and, with explicit language, provides a cognitive map for continuous growth and learning."

But what is the best way to make the Habits of Mind explicit and valued? What indicators should we choose to guide growth and improvement? And how do we best ensure continuous growth and learning? Costa and Kallick begin by placing the Habits of Mind at the center of assessment and give examples of what mature application of each of the Habits of Mind might look like. They describe specific behaviors that might be associated with a high-level application of each of the Habits of Mind and the kinds of evidence that would indicate students are acquiring the Habits of Mind.

They further suggest how we might recognize growth in a Habit of Mind by identifying these behaviors. For example, they say, "students demonstrate growth in persistence when they increase their use of alternative problem-solving strategies." Throughout the chapter, the Habits of Mind sit firmly in the spotlight.

Costa and Kallick continue by providing examples of different strategies that are commonly employed by schools to directly assess the Habits of Mind. These include checklists, rubrics, portfolios, reflection, and goal setting. Several "novice to expert" rubrics for the Habits of Mind are shared. Other tables that suggest measurement of the Habits of Mind in terms of the observable frequency with which students engage in the Habit of Mind from "not yet" to "sometimes" and ending with "frequently" are also provided.

What all these approaches have in common is that they focus on the Habit of Mind itself. And they seek to make explicit what quality application of the Habit of Mind looks like and then judge the degree to which students' actions match that definition.

The entire section, and the school-based examples used, which are still used today, reflects the dominant paradigm of the time for assessing the Habits of Mind. That the Habit of Mind be the *direct* and *explicit* focus of assessment. That we identify and describe specific behaviors associated with the Habit of Mind to make this assessment. And that the way to ensure continuous growth is to describe the progression of those behaviors. In short, that we should be seeking to answer the question, "how well developed are a student's Habits of Mind?"

While the assessment mechanisms described in 2008 are valuable and useful in specific contexts, they also present some challenges for assessing the Habits of Mind. In this chapter, we begin by exploring the shortfalls and challenges of this old paradigm. We then go on to describe a new approach to assessing the Habits of Mind, where instead of putting the Habits of Mind at the center, we place the *problem the Habits are looking to solve* at the center.

Additionally, instead of attempting to assess the Habits of Mind directly, we assess it indirectly based on the degree of success students achieve. Instead of asking how well-developed a student's Habits of Mind are, we asked are they *well enough* developed. Finally, we introduce the Habits of Mind Profile Tool, a game-changing way to assess and guide the development of your Habits of Mind.

SHORTFALLS AND CHALLENGES OF THE HISTORIC HABITS OF MIND PARADIGM

Challenges for Assessing Habits of Mind

One of the biggest challenges to assessing the Habits of Mind is that how we engage in a Habit of Mind is context sensitive. There are some broad-brush qualities relevant and useful in describing each of the Habits of Mind. However, in practice, the way we engage in a Habit of Mind is highly nuanced and specific depending on the context. For example, the specific strategies one would use to persist when writing a difficult email are very different to those used to persist when sticking to a specific diet. And both are different, again, to how you would persist when trying to reach a long-term goal.

Then there is the problem of transferability. Just because you can apply a Habit of Mind successfully in a context you're familiar with does not mean you'll be so successful applying it in an unfamiliar context. While the tendency toward engaging in particular Habits of Mind might be transferable, the specific skill set and ability to recognize when to call upon that Habit of Mind, the choice to do so, and your ability to self-assess within a context might not be so transferable. To say you are good at managing your impulsivity in one context does not necessarily mean you are good at managing your impulsivity in a different context!

The trade-off between specificity and transferability presents problems for designing assessment devices such as check lists or rubrics. If we make the device highly contextual and identify very specific behaviors, we lose the ability to transfer it to other contexts. If we make the qualities, we wish to observe very general, the device becomes more transferable. But the lack of specificity opens it up to subjective error as the qualities we are trying to observe become obscured in generalities.

By way of example, in the past schools have tried to assess Habits of Mind using what I refer to as "small rubrics." These sets of rules are highly detailed and relevant to a specific task. Small rubrics clearly identify specific behaviors associated with the application of the Habit, within a particular context.

For example, the relevant small rubric might identify a specific strategy, context, or outcome expected in a unit of work. In this type of rubric, the developmental increments between each level can be made small enough and specific enough to be easily recognized and assessed. The downside is that to make widespread use of this strategy requires the creation of dozens, if not hundreds, of rubrics that span every context, in every year level.

The alternative is to create "big rubrics." These are the novice to expert kind described by Costa and Kallick (2008). However, there are problems with these types as well. The issue here is not only that the descriptors used tend to be general and open to subjective error, but also that the development increments are so large as to lose their usefulness when trying to measure and facilitate continuous growth and improvement. Imagine how a standard five-level novice to expert rubric would be applied in a K-12 school. With 12 years of schooling, and five levels of progress, would students be expected to spend two years moving between levels?

Even the terms "novice to expert"—sometimes also called "low to high"—are problematic. For example, on an absolute scale, an eight-year-old is likely to have less well-developed Habits of Mind than an adult. Because of this, they would likely be described as a "novice," or their standard as "low." However, our eight-year-old might, in fact, be experiencing a great deal of success and have very highly developed Habits of Mind *compared to the level of difficulty they are facing.* They might, in fact, be excelling at school.

On the other hand, an adult might test quite highly against the absolute standards. But they may still be struggling and failing at the problems they are confronting. As we will discuss below, an individual's level of development is more meaningfully measured relative to the level of difficulty of the problems the person is facing, rather than trying to make assessments on an absolute scale.

The problems outlined above are only some of the issues facing traditional measures of assessing the Habits of Mind. Others include:

- The difficulty in accurately judging students' Habits of Mind. For example, can the behaviors be directly observed? If they can, how accurate will the judgment be?
- The accuracy of the comparison between the external standard and the observed behavior.
- The meaning of the closed end of the "expert" scale. (What does this mean anyway?)
- Understanding the pathway for development and growth beyond expert.

All these issues stem from trying to directly assess the Habit of Mind against an external set of criteria.

This approach, which has become the default way of trying to assess the Habits of Mind, reflects how we assess most things in schools. We establish a set of *absolute* standards (often arbitrarily) and then measure student progress against those standards. While this approach might be useful when assessing progress in language or mathematics, the approach described below offers many advantages for assessing the Habits of Mind.

THE NEW APPROACH TO ASSESSING
THE HABITS OF MIND

Defining Your WHY

In the old methodology, we put the Habit of Mind at the center of our assessment. The title on the rubric is the name of the Habit of Mind. We tell students that it is important to develop their Habits of Mind. In the minds of students, the Habit of Mind is in many ways a separate learning outcome—identified and assessed independently of the content being taught. But is this best way to approach the Habits of Mind, and in particular the assessment of the Habits of Mind?

In his book, *Start With Why*, Simon Sinek challenges us to identify our "why"—our purpose for doing what we do. Simon posits that people won't truly commit to an idea until they understand the WHY behind it. So, if we apply Sinek's thinking to our understanding of the Habits of Mind we are led to ask why students would ever engage with the Habits of Mind in the first place.

Under the old methodology, the "why" that is given to the students is largely about the Habits of Mind themselves. It's the behaviors associated with the Habits of Mind that are being measured. The Habits of Mind could almost be seen as important, detached in some way from the rest of classroom learning. In some schools the Habits of Mind are assessed and reported on independently, and it's possible to do well at an individual Habit of Mind, while doing poorly at the core work—or vice versa.

Of course, there is a connection between the Habit of Mind and the content learning, or the problems being solved, but this is not always clear or explicit, and students may feel that what's *really* important is the Habit itself. They might believe that the answer to the question, "Why are we doing Habits of Mind?" is "because the Habits of Mind themselves are important."

For most learners, the "why" isn't the Habits of Mind. Most learners are more focused on the problem and solving that problem. After all, it is the solution to the problem—the grade or the outcome—that is generally rewarded, both in school and in life. There is no reward for having well-developed Habits of Mind if the problem doesn't get solved.

Similarly, for some in our school community, the Habits of Mind are seen as an extra, or an add on, and hardly important at all. Consequently, it can be hard to get buy in from students or from teachers. But again, that changes when we make the problem our why.

I recall observing a lesson some years ago involving four and five-year-old students. The teacher began by explaining the problem that needed solving. The students were going to be doing an investigation into living things they could find around the school grounds. After explaining the task, the teacher asked the children, "Which of the Habits of Mind do you think *will help us in today's lesson?*" The teacher was establishing the WHY of the Habits of Mind first, which led to stronger student engagement. Putting the problem clearly at the center of our work dramatically increases the relevance of the Habits of Mind for students.

At the same school, there was a very high level of commitment toward the Habits of Mind from teachers. The Habits of Mind were seen as an integral way to help students achieve their learning goals. When curriculums focus on content-learning outcomes, specialist teachers see their job as teaching content, and students and parents are driven by content-learning outcomes. In this way the Habits of Mind become a means to an end—solving the problem. Consequently, we see a much greater level of commitment to the Habits of Mind.

In this paradigm we put the problem at the center. We develop our Habits of Mind, not for their sake themselves, but because they help us solve problems!

This provides a relevance and authenticity to the Habits of Mind that may have previously been lacking in the minds of students (and some teachers).

CHANGING THE PARADIGM FOR ASSESSMENT

The shift in paradigm that puts problems at the center transforms the way we think about and assess the Habits of Mind and provides a useful cognitive map for continuous growth. This shift begins with moving from an *absolute* measure of the Habits of Mind to a *relative* measure.

Consider the eight-year-old and the adult described above. Both are engaging in using the same Habit of Mind. The eight-year-old is experiencing success because their Habit of Mind is *well enough developed for the level of difficulty they are currently facing.* The adult, while their Habit of Mind might be more well developed on an absolute scale, is experiencing struggle. Their Habit of Mind *is not well enough developed for the level of difficulty they are currently facing.*

Why is this important? Because at the end of the day it doesn't matter how well developed your Habits of Mind are. What matters is if they are *well enough* developed for the challenges you're typically facing. If you're not succeeding at meeting the challenges you are currently facing, then you need to develop your Habits of Mind. If you *are* succeeding at the types of challenges you typically encounter, then it might be time to seek out new challenges! In this way we create a meaningful cognitive map for continuous growth. A map that, as we describe below, is driven by challenges that problems present!

This example illustrates the paradigm shift being proposed. We shift away from asking, "How well developed is your Habit of Mind?" toward a more meaningful, "Is your Habit of Mind well enough developed for the challenges you are currently facing?"

Assessing Individual Habits of Mind

It's worth noting that not all Habits of Mind are equally important to a given problem. Each problem can be thought of as having a unique Habits of Mind profile. Each Habit of Mind contributes a different degree of significance to a particular problem.

For example, when giving a speech Thinking and Communicating with Clarity and Precision is likely to be critical to successfully completing that problem. If that Habit is not executed well enough, there's likely to be significant negative impacts on performance. On the other hand, Remaining Open to

Continuous Learning is likely to be unimportant in the delivery of the speech (although it might be important to delivering a better speech next time).

We can leverage this relationship between the problem and specific Habits of Mind to indirectly assess the specific Habit of Mind. By focusing on the problems where a Habit of Mind is critical and assessing the degree of success that we experience when confronting a problem, we can answer the question, "Is that habit of mind well enough developed to allow you to succeed at the problems you're facing?" The degree of success we experience when confronted with a problem where a Habit of Mind is critical to the solution of that problem becomes a proxy for assessing that Habit of Mind.

Further, when focusing on the problem we usually have clearly defined and authentic indicators to measure the degree of success that we experience. There's no need to come up with additional criteria for each of the Habits of Mind. This vastly simplifies assessment as we don't need to come up with yet another set of assessment criteria for each Habit of Mind in each context.

Finally, by defining the "degree of success" in transferable terms, we can make this approach applicable to any problem, in any context, at every year level in the school. For example, excelling at any problem would mean reaching or exceeding all the intended outcomes, to an extremely high standard, completed within all constraints with close to an error-free performance.

Assessing our Habits of Mind relative to the level of difficulty of the problems we are currently facing has two powerful purposes.

1. It provides genuine motivation for growth by defining a purpose for development and identifying our "why."
2. It offers a unique, genuine, and powerful way to ensure continuous growth and improvement.

Challenge: Your Pathway for Development

Without challenge there can be no growth. We can't independently develop Habits of Mind in the absence of challenges. In fact, challenges provide both the reason and the mechanism to develop our Habits of Mind. A challenge produces the gap between our current abilities and the ones we need. The mistakes and struggle produced as part of challenge provide the raw material for growth.

Excelling is not a sign for celebration or complacency. It's a sign that it's time to take on new challenges. As the world's expertise expert Anders Ericsson says, "It is a fundamental truth of any sort of practice, that if you never step outside your comfort zone, you will never grow."

Consider again the example above of the eight-year-old child. Currently, when they encounter problems where a Habit of Mind is critical, they excel.

That Habit of Mind is well enough developed *for their current level of challenge*. In reality, these problems are no longer challenging at all. They are simply in their comfort zone. The message, therefore, is that to drive continuous growth it's time to step outside your comfort zone and into your learning zone and take on greater challenges!

On the other hand, the adult in the example above *is* challenging themselves. They have stepped beyond their current abilities into their learning zone. This is where effort and struggle occur. It's where we make mistakes. And, ultimately, it's where growth takes place.

By putting the problem at the center and by asking, "Are our Habits of Mind well enough developed," we address the key issues of assessment raised by Costa and Kallick. We clearly identify the value of the Habits of Mind when we make specific, targeted Habits of Mind an explicit part of the problem-solving process. The indicators for observing growth and improvement are the tangible results we achieve as we succeed at increasingly difficult problems. And challenge provides the impetus for continuous growth and learning.

By asking the question, "Are our Habits of Mind well enough developed for the problems we regularly encounter?" we immediately address the problem of context. Context is automatically built into our assessment. All we need to do is identify problems that we regularly encounter where the Habit of Mind is critical to success.

When we put our problems at the center, the assessment strategy we develop is immediately transferable to any problem. By using the degree of success, we achieve at solving a problem as our measure of development, we can transfer the strategy into any context, and any level of development. The issues common to the use of both big and small rubrics disappear.

By creating a scale that is relative to our current level of challenge, rather than relative to an absolute scale that describes the Habit of Mind, we resolve the closed-end problem of the novice to expert scale, providing a clear path to continuous development. And by using authentic and objective assessment criteria related to the challenge we are confronting, we remove the need to create a second subjective assessment scale for the Habit of Mind.

Given the clear benefits of putting the problem at the center of our assessment, and making our assessment relative rather than absolute, how then do we create a tool to assess the Habits of Mind?

THE HABITS OF MIND PROFILE TOOL

The Habits of Mind Profile Tool is a unique, powerful, and practical online tool. It allows educators to assess learners' Habits of Mind, and to provide guidance for ongoing growth and development. It is easily completed by asking a simple question related to each of the Habits of Mind:

As you consider problems that you regularly encounter, where this Habit of Mind is critical to success, what results do you tend to get?

The response is measured on a scale from excel, achieve, complete, struggle, fail, or avoid. Judgement is based on a single rubric that describes the degree to which the authentic outcomes of the problems are met. The degree of success achieved is used to determine the degree of development, relative to the level of challenge. This is then translated to identify if the individual is working with that Habit of Mind in their comfort zone, performance zone, learning zone or zone of concern (well beyond their current abilities).

Accuracy of the Habits of Mind Profile Tool is increased by allowing multiple people to contribute to the assessment. For example, a profile might be created by combining the judgement of a learner, a teacher, and a parent. Or by combining the judgments of an employee, a colleague, and a supervisor.

An individual Habits of Mind profile is then produced that provides a snapshot of the individual's Habits of Mind as shown in Figure 14.1. The Habits are ranked in order of development and assessed relative to the difficulty of the problems regularly encountered. The Habits are further grouped by the zone of learning they fall into.

This highly visual tool provides both an assessment of the individual's Habits of Mind, as well as a course of action for future development.

When Habits of Mind appear in the comfort zone (orange) this identifies a relative strength. Problems that are regularly encountered where this Habit of Mind is critical are easily completed, to a very high standard, with all outcomes met or exceeded. The individual could be described as "cruising" in regard to these types of challenges. This speaks to the need to seek out new challenges.

When Habits of Mind appear in the performance zone (blue) this represents a well-developed Habit of Mind. Problems that are regularly encountered where this Habit of Mind is critical are completed to a high standard. A decision needs to be made at this point if further consolidation is desirable and new challenges found to facilitate growth, or if the level of development is sufficient for now, and resources invested in developing other Habits of Mind.

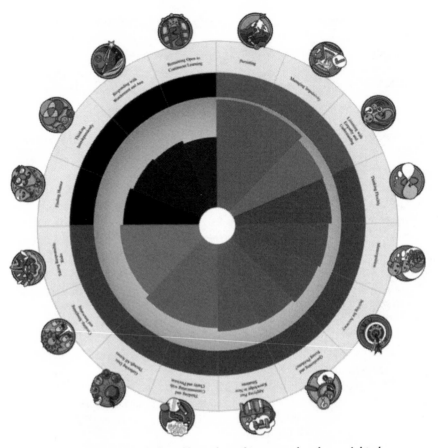

Figure 14.1. The Habits of Mind Profile Tool. *Author created and copyrighted.*

Habits of Mind that appear in the learning zone (green) is where growth happens and should be the major focus for learning. Counterintuitively, our goal is not to get all a learner's Habits of Mind in the orange zone, but to keep the profile largely (though not entirely) in the green. They should be regularly challenging themselves, and frequently moving Habits out of areas of blue and orange. To focus on the habits in our learning zone is to focus on growth. In classroom settings it is a "green" profile that is valued most highly, not an orange one.

The Habits of Mind profile allows you can gain insights into a learner's Habits of Mind at a glance. It shows which Habits of Mind they are working on and where they need to be challenged. And by identifying the dominant color of a profile we can see how they are working overall.

For example, a largely orange profile represents a student that is coasting and not being challenged. A blue profile is a student who is doing well but may be stuck in a performance mode—doing their best without getting better. A profile that shows a lot of red represents a student that is overly stretched, operating in an environment that poses too great a challenge.

When a Habit of Mind is in our learning zone, we draw on our understanding of the Dimensions of Growth discussed in chapter 11 to guide our development. The degree to which this development is driven by the teacher or is more self-directed will depend on the individual. Development is guided by seeking to develop a deeper understanding of the meaning of that Habit of Mind by:

- Increasing the repertoire of strategies at the learner's disposal
- Becoming more alert to the cues, signals, and indicators that alert the learner to opportunities to engage in that Habit of Mind
- Being more attuned to the benefits that arise from engaging in the Habit of Mind
- Improving their ability to self-direct, self-assess, and self-manage the development of the Habit of Mind
- Focusing on the context the learner is operating in

Note that looking at the profile does not tell you anything about how well-developed a person's Habits of Mind are on an absolute scale. Only how well-developed they are in relation to the problems they regularly encounter. The profile is focused on growth, and identifying actions to achieve further growth, rather than on absolute standards. This is a powerful asset as it means interpreting a profile and the actions that follow are as relevant to an eight-year-old child as it is to an adult.

A Habits of Mind profile not only drives growth by identifying when to take on greater challenge, it also allows us to track growth and development over time. By comparing profiles that were taken at different times you can track the "rise and fall" of Habits of Mind as the learner stretches to more challenging environments. The learner will push a Habit of Mind "down" into the green, then work on developing the Habit of Mind to bring it up again into blue and orange before repeating the process of seeking out new challenges to facilitate further growth.

Habits of Mind Problem Profile

It's possible to create a Habits of Mind *problem* profile. This type of profile identifies the relative importance of each Habit of Mind to a particular problem. This is a powerful tool, which helps learners to identify the Habits of Mind that are going to be beneficial to solving a particular problem. A problem profile provides similar information to the profile examples above, but here the teacher identifies the Habits of Mind that are going to be most important to the problem-solving process.

By comparing a learner's personal Habits of Mind profile to a problem profile, it becomes possible to create a personalized problem profile. This is one that shows the amount of stretch and challenge that will be provided by a particular problem for each learner.

For example, if the problem profile indicated that Striving for Accuracy was critical to a particular problem, and a learner's personal profile indicated that this Habit of Mind was not well developed, the personalised problem profile would highlight this level of stretch. This is particularly powerful, as it identifies beforehand the aspects of the challenge that will need to be a focus for each learner.

Creating Your Habits of Mind Profile

The Habits of Mind Profile Tool is an online tool that can be accessed from habitsofmind.jamesanderson.com.au. The free online version allows you to create a personal Habits of Mind profile, with one contributor. The paid version can be customized to specific school needs, and can create personal profiles with multiple contributors, as well as problem profiles and individualized problem profiles and can manage and store profiles for students over time.

SUMMARY

For many years, the assessment of learners' Habits of Mind has followed a traditional model that puts the Habits at the center and seeks to directly assess the Habits of Mind against an external and absolute set of criteria. It attempted to answer the question of "how well developed" the learners' Habits of Mind are.

This new tool offers a powerful new alternative by asking the question are the learners Habits of Mind "well enough developed" to succeed at problems the learner regularly encounters. The Habits of Mind Profile Tool that answers this question can be consistently applied across year levels and subject areas to drive continuous reflection and development of the Habits of Mind.

Putting the problem at the center of assessment creates relevance and purpose, improving both teacher and learner buy-in. And the highly visual nature of the Habits of Mind profile allows learners and teachers alike to make insightful and intuitive judgments.

REFERENCES

Costa, A., & Kallick, B. (2008). *Learning and leading with Habits of Mind: 16 essential characteristics for success.* Alexandria, VA. ASCD.

Sinek, S. (2011). *Start with why: How great leaders inspire everyone to take action.* Penguin (General UK).

Ericsson, A., & Pool, R. (2016). *Peak: Secrets from the new science of expertise.* HarperOne.

About the Editors and Authors

Servet Altan is an assistant professor within the faculty of education at MEF University. He is currently the academic coordinator for IB Programmes at MEF University. He earned his PhD in curriculum and instruction from Bilkent University. He is a Leader IB Educator and he has several active roles in the IBO (International Baccalaureate Organization). He is an internationally known teacher educator and he continues his research on Habits of Mind and motivation.

Jennie Lane is an associate professor within the Graduate School of Education at Bilkent University. She received her BS in biology from Florida Southern College and Master's degrees from Columbia Teachers College and the University of Wisconsin–Stevens Point. She earned her PhD in curriculum and instruction from UW–Madison. Prior to coming to Bilkent in 2012, she was the director of the Wisconsin K-12 Energy Education Program (KEEP) for 17 years. Her other work experience includes co-authoring the *Project WET Curriculum and Activity Guide* which is used throughout the world, teaching public school in New York City and Lewiston, and instructing pre-service teachers in Thailand and at the University of Wisconsin–Stevens Point. She has published papers in the *Journal of Environmental Education, Energy Policy, Environmental Education Research*, and other journals. Her research areas include environmental, place-based, and sustainability education.

Allison Zmuda works with educators to grow ideas on how to make learning for students challenging, possible, and worthy of the attempt. Over the past 20 years, Zmuda has shared curricular, assessment, and instructional ideas, shown illustrative examples, and offered practical strategies of how to get started. She co-authored *Students at the Center: Personalized Learning with Habits of Mind* with Bena Kallick. She is co-director of the Institute for Habits of Mind.

Arthur L. Costa is a past president of ASCD, author, and editor of books and articles including *Cognitive Coaching* (with Robert Garmston), *The School as Home for the Mind, Developing Minds: A Resource Book for Teaching Thinking*, and many books on Habits of Mind (with Bena Kallick) such as the recently published *Nurturing Habits of Mind in Early Childhood Classrooms*. He is co-founder and director of the Institute for Habits of Mind.

Bena Kallick is an author, speaker, and educational consultant who has co-authored many books on Habits of Mind with Arthur Costa. She also co-authored *Students at the Center: Personalized Learning with Habits of Mind* with Allison Zmuda. She is co-founder and director of the Institute for Habits of Mind.

Daniel Vollrath, EdD, is a special education teacher and professional developer for the Institute for Habits of Mind. Daniel received his doctorate in special education leadership from Arcadia University. He provides services and support to schools dedicated to bringing the Habits of Mind into their culture and community. Daniel has spoken at many conferences, such as the first-ever National Principals Conference and the 2019 ASCD Conference on Teaching for Excellence.

David Bauzá-Capart has been working in leadership positions in international schools for the last 20 years. He is a lead educator for the International Baccalaureate and has held several roles for the IB Educator Network. He completed his EdD from the Fundación Universitaria Iberoamericana (Puerto Rico, USA). David has written for the *International School Magazine* and has provided professional development sessions on diverse topics related to education.

Erika Elkady has been working in international baccalaureate (IB) schools for over 25 years. Erika has held several roles for the IB Educator Network over the past 15 years. She has written for GL Education, the *International School Leader Magazine*, and ISC Research. She has provided presentations for the IB, KHDA, and the University of Birmingham as well as GL Education on the topic of student well-being through character education.

James Anderson is a speaker, author, and educator, with more than 25 years of experience working with the Habits of Mind. His books include *Succeeding with Habits of Mind*, as well as *The Agile Learner* and *The Learning Landscape*, where he extends and deepens our understanding of the Habits of Mind by skillfully weaving them with Dweck's work on growth mindset and Ericsson's work on deliberate practice to create the concept of Learnership.

Jennifer L. Edwards, PhD, serves as professor in the leadership for change doctoral program in the School of Leadership Studies for Fielding Graduate University in Santa Barbara, CA. She has written *Research on Habits of Mind* (Institute for Habits of Mind International, 2014) and *Inviting Students to Learn: 100 Tips for Talking Effectively with Your Students* (ASCD, 2010).

Jody S. Piro, EdD, is a professor in the doctor of education in instructional leadership program at Western Connecticut State University. She holds an EdD in curriculum leadership from Northern Illinois University. Jody has published peer-reviewed articles in many esteemed teacher education journals. She authored the book *10 Dilemmas in Teaching with Discussion: Managing Integral Instruction.*

Julio Vazquez, EdD, is the director of instruction and human resources in the North Salem Central School District in North Salem, New York. He obtained his doctorate in educational leadership at Western Connecticut State University. Julio has given many presentations about enabling student, teacher, and administrator success and developing students' Habits of Mind, critical and creative thinking, and problem-solving abilities.

Nick Bruski, EdD, has served in various positions in education including classroom teaching, coaching, administration, training, and higher education. He completed his doctor of education degree at UCLA. Nick continues to serve in public education as a leader of an International Habits of the Mind Elementary School and provides consulting services for teacher evaluation, school culture and growth, curriculum, and leadership.

Philip G. Muscott has worked within K-12 education for the past 20 years after transitioning from the financial services sector. His areas of expertise are in the Understanding by Design framework for curriculum planning, the 16 Habits of Mind and Personalized Learning, where he actively engages in delivering professional development, and designing curriculum within these frameworks. Philip currently chairs the International Habits of Mind Research Community.

Priscila Freitas Torres earned a master's degree in international education from Framingham State University, and graduate degrees in neurological development from University of Brasília, Brazil, and leadership and supervision with a focus on technology from Johns Hopkins University. She is the head of school of Escola Concept São Paulo, Brazil. She also serves as a business unit director at the corporate level of the Grupo SEB educational group.

William A. Sommers, PhD, is a learner, teacher, principal, author, leadership coach, and consultant. He has served as an adjunct faculty member at Texas State University, Hamline University, University of St. Thomas, St. Mary's University, Union Institute, and Capella University. He has co-authored an ebook called *Trainer's Companion for Habits of Mind*, 2nd ed. (2015).